Praise for
Emotional Intelligence for Managing Results in a Diverse World

"Offers a vision of how we should understand ourselves and others. The information and questions presented are amazingly effective at helping people connect. Our global society is in need of this type of awakening, understanding, and training."

—Timothy E. Findley, EdD, MBA, Division Director, Diversity and Inclusion, Norton Healthcare

"Makes the topic of emotional intelligence and diversity accessible to all and easily applied in the workplace, at all levels of an organization. The authors have mastered the art of educating us about how best to manage our emotions in a diverse world and use them to build positive working relationships."

—Robert C. Amelio, Vice President, Diversity and Talent Management, Dana-Farber Cancer Institute

"I would recommend this book to anyone who is interested in and willing to take the risk and opportunity to discover their own strengths and weaknesses, beliefs and biases, and values and fears, for the purpose of becoming a better person, communicator, and manager."

—Linda C. Avila, Director, UCLA Staff Affirmative Action Office

"All I have to say is, 'Wow, this book is a home run.' I will make this required reading for my management staff as we strive to increase team effectiveness and performance through emotional intelligence—and also serve our external customers through a better understanding of their needs and wants."

—Tony Jenkins, Market President, Blue Cross Blue Shield of Florida

Emotional Intelligence
for Managing Results in a Diverse World

Emotional Intelligence
for Managing Results
in a Diverse World

The Hard Truth About Soft Skills in the Workplace

Lee Gardenswartz
Jorge Cherbosque
Anita Rowe

Davies-Black Publishing
Mountain View, California

Published by Davies-Black Publishing, a division of CPP, Inc., 1055 Joaquin Road, 2nd Floor, Mountain View, CA 94043; 800-624-1765.

Special discounts on bulk quantities of Davies-Black books are available to corporations, professional associations, and other organizations. For details, contact the Director of Marketing and Sales at Davies-Black Publishing: 650-691-9123; fax 650-623-9271.

Visit the Davies-Black Publishing Web site at www.daviesblack.com.

Printed in the United States of America
12 11 10 09 08   10 9 8 7 6 5 4 3 2 1

Library of Congress Cataloging-in-Publication Data

Gardenswartz, Lee.
    Emotional intelligence for managing results in a diverse world : the hard truth about soft skills in the workplace / Lee Gardenswartz, Jorge Cherbosque, Anita Rowe.
        p. cm.

Includes bibliographical references and index.
ISBN 978-0-89106-255-4 (hardcover)
1. Diversity in the workplace. 2. Emotional intelligence. I. Cherbosque, Jorge. II. Rowe, Anita. III. Title.

HF5549.5.M5G365 2008

658.4'094—dc22

2008015766

FIRST EDITION
First printing 2008

Contents

Activities, Checklists, Figures, Table

Activities

Checklists

Figures

Table

About the Authors

Lee Gardenswartz, PhD, is a partner in the Emotional Intelligence and Diversity Institute (EIDI) and in the management consulting firm of Gardenswartz & Rowe of Los Angeles, California. Since 1980 Gardenswartz & Rowe has specialized in shaping corporate culture for a variety of clients across the country, helping them build productive and cohesive work teams and create intercultural understanding and harmony in the workplace.

In addition to working directly with clients, Gardenswartz and her partner, Anita Rowe, have also helped organizations through their writing on diversity. They have coauthored books such as *Managing Diversity: A Complete Desk Reference and Planning Guide* (1993; revised edition, 1998), which won the Book of the Year award from the Society for Human Resource Management (SHRM), and has served as a primary guide to organizations in structuring their diversity initiatives, providing not only conceptual information but techniques and tools as well. Gardenswartz and Rowe have coauthored *The Managing Diversity Survival Guide* (1994), *The Diversity Tool Kit* (1994), *Diverse Teams at Work* (1995), *Managing Diversity in Health Care* (1998), *Managing Diversity in Health Care Manual* (1999), and *The Global Diversity Desk Reference* (2003).

Among Gardenswartz & Rowe's clients are Sempra Energy, Harvard Medical School, Shell Oil Company, the Internal Revenue Service, Kaiser Permanente, the American Broadcasting Company, the Boeing Company, Equity

Residential, Countrywide Financial Corporation, Wells Fargo, Walt Disney World, Starbucks, Cox Communications, and Progress Energy. Gardenswartz & Rowe's principals also continue to teach about diversity through SHRM's Diversity Train-the-Trainer certificate program and through institutions such as the Summer Institute for Intercultural Communication in Portland, Oregon, and the Emotional Intelligence and Diversity Institute.

Jorge Cherbosque, PhD, has codirected the University of California at Los Angeles (UCLA) Staff and Faculty Counseling and Consultation Center for the past seventeen years. He also teaches at the Anderson School of Management at UCLA.

Cherbosque is a speaker, trainer, and consultant for various clients, including Cox Communications, Knight Ryder Digital, Chase Manhattan Bank, Verizon, Neutrogena, and General Motors. He has also served as a resource for the Young Presidents Organization (YPO), the Young Entrepreneur Organization (YEO), and the World Presidents Organization (WPO). Known as an expert in Hispanic marketing, he has moderated numerous qualitative studies for clients such as General Motors, Ford Motor Company, Verizon, Wells Fargo, Target, and Toyota.

Cherbosque has published articles in a broad range of scholarly journals. He is also in demand as a keynote speaker and a workshop presenter on topics such as "Moving from the Ordinary to the Extraordinary," "Discovering the Hidden Treasures of Your Family," and "Emotional Intelligence as a Leadership Skill that Inspires Heart and Soul Commitment."

Anita Rowe, PhD, partner in Gardenswartz & Rowe and the Emotional Intelligence and Diversity Institute, has been consulting with organizations regarding diversity since 1977, helping them manage culture change, build productive and cohesive work teams, and create intercultural understanding and harmony in the workplace. She holds a doctorate of human behavior from the United States International University.

In addition to direct client relationships, Rowe and her partner, Lee Gardenswartz, have also helped organizations through their writing on diversity. They have coauthored books such as *Managing Diversity: A Complete Desk Reference and Planning Guide* (1993; revised edition, 1998) which won the

Book of the Year award from the Society for Human Resource Management, and has served as a primary guide to organizations in structuring their diversity initiatives, providing not only conceptual information but techniques and tools as well. Rowe and Gardenswartz have coauthored *The Managing Diversity Survival Guide* (1994), *The Diversity Tool Kit* (1994), *Diverse Teams at Work* (1995), *Managing Diversity in Health Care* (1998), *Managing Diversity in Health Care Manual* (1999), and *The Global Diversity Desk Reference* (2003).

Among Gardenswartz & Rowe's clients are Sempra Energy, Harvard Medical School, Shell Oil Company, the Internal Revenue Service, Kaiser Permanente, the American Broadcasting Company, the Boeing Company, Equity Residential, Countrywide Financial Corporation, Wells Fargo, Walt Disney World, Starbucks, Cox Communications, and Progress Energy. Gardenswartz & Rowe's principals also continue to teach about diversity through SHRM's Diversity Train-the-Trainer certificate program and through institutions such as the Summer Institute for Intercultural Communication in Portland, Oregon, and the Emotional Intelligence and Diversity Institute.

Introduction

Over the past decade, emotional intelligence has come to be seen more and more as a critical underpinning of success on and off the job. It has become even more important as work environments have become increasingly diverse and have brought together differences that can be challenging. However, despite its importance, most individuals haven't been taught how to develop this aspect of themselves. It is not part of the three Rs in school, and most people are not given the methods and tools to deal with feelings that are critical to effectiveness in work, relationships, and life.

The good news is that emotional intelligence is a competency that can be learned. Although some people may have a greater natural affinity for dealing with feelings, no matter how gifted or underendowed you may be in this area, you can develop the skills and improve your ability to understand and deal effectively with feelings, your own and those of others, especially when differences trigger emotional responses.

One purpose of this book is to give you the fundamentals of emotional intelligence, the understanding and the tools to function effectively in the emotional landscape of your diverse work world. Whether you are a manager, human resources professional, organization development consultant, trainer, diversity director, coach, or team leader, this book will give you both a mirror and a map to increase your own competence in managing emotions. It will also give you the know-how to use this knowledge and approach in coaching and developing others to help them be more successful on the job. The mirror comes in the form of tools and processes that show you how to take some good, hard, and honest looks at yourself in order to understand your motivations, feelings, reactions, and behaviors at a deeper level. This is essential because, as one of our best teachers, author and organization development consultant John E. Jones, said, "Awareness precedes choice." Before you can make effective choices about how to respond and act, you need to understand yourself and your situations clearly and honestly. Just understanding yourself is not enough, though. Renowned psychologist Dr. William Glasser is reputed to have quipped many years ago that "awareness and 50 cents gets you a cup of coffee." While that cup of java costs more today, it still holds true that all the awareness in the world without action won't get you very far. This book also provides the map in the form of activities and tools that give you guidance in creating ways to cope and respond more effectively to the emotional content of daily situations on the job. Together the mirrors and the maps will provide you with the keys to increase your own emotional intelligence in a diverse environment so you can experience greater internal peace and external success. If you are responsible for guiding others, these tools will enable you to help them increase their success as well.

Chapter 1 explains how emotions matter in the workplace and why learning to understand and manage emotions is a key to your effectiveness. Chapter 2 goes on to show you how the differences diversity brings can trigger emotions, and it presents the Emotional Intelligence and Diversity Model as a way to understand and deal with those feelings. Chapters 3, 4, 5, and 6 explain the dimensions of emotional intelligence and diversity, providing examples, activities, and methods to increase your competence in each dimension. The last two chapters, Chapters 7 and 8, give you specific maps, actions to take to help individual staff members and teams develop competence in these areas.

You will learn more from this book if you are an active participant in this journey, not a just a passive reader. You will be asked questions, challenged to examine yourself, stimulated to expand your thinking, and encouraged to take action to apply the concepts you are learning as you read. Doing so will make this journey a valuable one for you, a journey that has a real payoff in effectiveness in your work world and beyond. Bon voyage!

1

You Can't Leave Your Feelings at Home

Emotions aren't just touchy-feely things that belong in a therapy session. Nor are they aspects of yourself—or of others—that need to be hidden, ashamed of, or ignored. They are a legitimate and powerful part of you and your relationships. They are also the energy behind behavior, whether it is yours or that of others. What's more important, how you deal with those emotions results in consequences, leading to both your successes and your failures. Human beings function on both rational and emotional levels, and emotions are at the heart of energy, commitment, and motivation. Despite the old adage that you should "leave your feelings at home," emotions come to work along with your thoughts. You know the exhilaration and energy you feel when you are doing work that matters to you. You remember the excitement and anticipation you felt at the beginning of a promising new job or assignment. On the other hand, you probably also recall the knot in your stomach when you made a major error at work, or the anxiety and dread you felt when you had a conflict looming with a boss, colleague, or subordinate.

Although emotions are the source of engagement, joy, and energy, they are also at the heart of anger, frustration, and disengagement. Feelings are there, whether you like it or not. If you don't acknowledge and manage them, they'll be managing you, your relationships, and your workplace environment. Without the ability to understand and deal with emotions effectively, you will continue to undermine your chances for effectiveness.

Emotional intelligence is the ability to understand and deal with feelings, both your own and those of others, in a healthy and constructive way. Your ability to be effective in today's diverse world, on and off the job, depends on it. When you have the tools to harness the power of emotions, you can build energized, engaged, and productive teams. If not, emotions will manage your interactions, your work group, and its output.

Emotional Intelligence Affects Profitability and Performance

In the past few years, thanks to the work of Daniel Goleman and others, acknowledgment and understanding of the essential role emotions play in shaping a person's success have been growing. Most people would agree that IQ has never been enough to be successful and fulfilled in life. Who can't point to colleagues and friends who are off the charts in intellectual gifts yet are their own worst enemies because their emotional intelligence doesn't match their IQ. According to the Center for Creative Leadership, the three most significant causes of career derailment for executives involve deficits in emotional competence:

- Difficulty handling change
- Inability to work in a team
- Poor interpersonal relations

Feelings and the impact they have can even be quantified. According to Tony Simons, writing in the *Harvard Business Review*, the more employees feel trust—an emotional response—in their bosses, the higher the profits for the organization. In one study, a one-eighth-point improvement on a survey of employees' perceptions of how much managers earned their confidence increased profitability by 2.5 percent; that increase in profitability meant a quarter of a million dollar profit increase per business unit per year.[1]

Additional research correlates emotional intelligence and performance:

- In a multinational consulting firm, partners who scored above the median in emotional intelligence competencies delivered $1.2 million more in profit from their accounts than did other partners, a 139 percent incremental gain.[2]

- At L'Oréal, salespeople selected on the basis of emotional competencies sold $91,370 more than other salespeople, for a net revenue increase of $2,558,360. They also had 63 percent less turnover in the first year.[3]

- After supervisors in a manufacturing plant received training in emotional competencies, accidents resulting in lost time decreased by 50 percent, formal grievances dropped from fifteen to three a year, and the plant exceeded production goals by $250,000.[4]

As you can see from these examples, feelings and the ability to deal with them have an impact on the bottom line. That is just the tip of the iceberg of the truth about soft skills.

The Power of Emotions in Dealing with Diversity

Although emotions have always been a significant factor in performance at work, the role they play is even greater in today's diverse work environments, where there is an increasingly wide array of cultures, lifestyles, and needs. You have undoubtedly experienced situations at work where you have seen the impact of feelings that result from dealing with diversity. You have also seen how the situations were dealt with, both effectively and ineffectively. Here are a few real-world examples.

- A CEO was confused and upset when one of her best manufacturing employees, a recent immigrant, quit unexpectedly. After investigating, she found out that the employee resigned because of a cultural difference. The shame and loss of face the employee experienced in a feedback session with her was what led to his departure.

- An executive understood the fear that was at the heart of his staff's resistance to the changes he had instituted regarding diversity. He therefore gave them a chance to vent their frustrations at an all-hands meeting where he could listen, show empathy, and then respond to their concerns. His response calmed their anxiety and enabled them to accept the changes and move on.

▪ A team leader was exasperated because his team members said yes to everything he asked and indicated that they understood, but they continued to make mistakes that made it clear that they did not understand. His frustration led to blowups on the plant floor that could have been avoided with some knowledge about cross-cultural communication.

Feelings are a fundamental part of your reactions to the differences you see in others, whether you approach or avoid them, like or dislike them, accept or reject them. In your workplace, it's probably not uncommon for workers from five generations, with multiple languages and a wide variety of backgrounds, styles, and values, to come together on the job. You may be intrigued and stimulated by these differences. However, you may also find that bruised feelings, volatile reactions, and unintentional disrespect can also be the result. Emotional intelligence is needed to deal with situations such as accusations of racism or sexism, splintering of work teams into ethnic factions, disengagement because of perceived lack of respect, claims of reverse discrimination, or divisions of "us versus them" on the staff. Your ability to admit and understand your own feelings about these issues brings a calming influence to the situation and helps you respond in an appropriate and effective way. It also helps you serve as a role model, demonstrating to staff ways to respond to emotionally charged situations in a healthy and productive manner.

Think of the feelings that might be triggered for you when differences arise in situations such as these:

▪ As the youngest employee on the team, you notice that a colleague does not include you when he recognizes all the contributors on an important project you worked on.

▪ A customer calls and complains about one of your staff members, saying, "I would never trust a person with a diamond in her nose. It's so unprofessional."

▪ A group of co-workers who have a different time orientation are consistently late to staff meetings, causing you and others to waste valuable time waiting.

▪ A client complains about your team members who have accents, saying, "Why don't you hire anyone who speaks English?"

■ At after-work happy hours, a number of your work associates make comments with racist, sexist, or homophobic undertones, saying they mean no harm and are just joking.

Feelings such as embarrassment, disgust, anger, indignation, frustration, and anxiety are not uncommon in situations such as these. Whatever the emotional responses are, they have consequences on the job, for both relationships and productivity. What do you and others do when these feelings emerge? Do you withdraw, confront, avoid, joke, problem-solve, use sarcasm, or verbally attack? Do your reactions help or hinder? Your feelings and the ensuing response have an impact in the workplace. When you acknowledge, understand, and manage your feelings, your behavior can be effective and productive. When you do not, counterproductive, even destructive, behavior can result. The diversity-related incidents in the stories that follow show what can happen when emotional intelligence is at work and when it is not.

The "Jewish Comment"

In the break room a group of co-workers were chatting about how expensive a particular item was. One of the group, Deborah, said she'd never spend that much on the item. Her co-worker Judy then asked if it was because she was Jewish. Hurt and appalled at the insensitive comment, Deborah did not respond. Instead she stopped talking to Judy, ruminated on her hurt, and after a few months of increasing disengagement, resigned from the staff. Judy never knew why Deborah stopped talking to her. The boss, knowing nothing about the incident, was shocked at the resignation, since Deborah had always been a productive and positive team member.

As you can see, emotions were in play, sabotaging not only relationships and teamwork but hindering careers as well. Had Deborah been able to understand and manage her feelings, she might have been able to respond differently. She could have asked Judy what she meant, expressed to her that the comment was hurtful, and explained how erroneous this underlying stereotype was. However, none of these responses were possible because Deborah was held captive by her emotional response to Judy's comment.

The Transgendered Employee

A manager was caught off guard when she was approached by one of her team members, a man who told her he was about to undergo the transgender process. The team member wanted her to know because he understood that this change would have repercussions in the work group. At first the manager felt uncomfortable, unsure of how to respond and extremely nervous when she thought about dealing with a situation for which she had no experience or training. However, after acknowledging her feelings, she thought about her options and realized that she did have the skills and tools to deal with the situation. It dawned on her that this employee was a human being in need, a person who had great relationships with his peers. So she asked him if he would be willing to share information about his situation with his co-workers and have a discussion with them about what was ahead for him. He agreed gladly, and she called a special team meeting at which he explained the process he would be going through and answered their questions candidly.

The most heartening aspect of this story is the team's support of the team member through the transition. Not only were his co-workers there for him through the emotional roller coaster of the change, but they served as ambassadors to the rest of the organization, explaining, dispelling myths, and helping others understand what was going on so that this employee could continue to work in a safe and supportive environment. Because the manager was able to understand her own feelings and those of her staff members, she could deal with them and respond in an effective way.

More often than not, when these kinds of difficult, emotionally charged situations arise, the discomfort they trigger causes people to sweep them under the rug. Avoiding the elephant in the room is a common way to manage the discomfort, yet hiding doesn't help in the long run. The issue or potential problem bubbles, brews, and usually escalates. However, with the skills of emotional intelligence, you can recognize the discomfort, understand it, and overcome the urge to avoid it so you can manage the situation effectively.

Think about times when you have been held hostage by your feelings and then responded in ineffective ways. Perhaps you lashed out, withdrew, said something you wished you hadn't, or made a poor decision. Think about times when you have been able to admit, understand, and manage your emotions so that you could take positive action. When have you seen your colleagues and staff members do both?

> *You can buy people's time; you can buy their physical presence at a given place; you can even buy a measured number of muscular motions per hour. But you cannot buy the devotions of their hearts. This you must earn.*
>
> —CLARENCE FRANCIS,
> Former CEO, General Foods Corporation

Emotional intelligence can pay big dividends in helping you succeed in your diverse workplace by giving you ways to deal effectively with situations like these. On Checklist 1 check which of the benefits you would like more of in your life.

Capturing and Using the Energy of Emotions

It has been said that if people could tap the power of emotions, they would never run out of energy. In order to be able to tap that power, you need to acknowledge and understand some realities about feelings and how they work in your life and in your organization. When you don't acknowledge, understand, and express your feelings, you not only have negative workplace consequences, you may find that the feelings are turned inward, leading to dysfunctional behaviors such as substance abuse and depression. As you read about these realities, consider how they relate to your situation.

Feelings Tell Us What Matters

Whenever you have a feeling reaction, whether it's exhilaration or fear, confusion or confidence, joy or deflation, something important has been tapped. Perhaps you are angry that a deeply held value of yours has been disregarded, ashamed because you didn't live up to one of your expectations for yourself, or thrilled because your sense of yourself was validated. It is important to

Checklist 1

Benefits of Increasing Emotional Intelligence in a Diverse World

FOR YOU . . .

☐ Increased self-confidence

☐ Decreased stress and worry

☐ Enhanced satisfaction at work

☐ Increased joy and laughter in life

☐ Reduced frustration

☐ More constructive ways of dealing with anger

☐ Smoother, more harmonious relationships

☐ Better cooperation from others

☐ An end to getting "hooked" by others

☐ A feeling of being more in control of your environment

☐ Increased understanding of others

☐ Ability to take more healthy risks

☐ Ability to let go of unrealistic expectations

☐ Increased skill in handling difficult conversations

☐ Better ways of dealing with the egos of others

FOR YOUR ORGANIZATION . . .

☐ Increased teamwork

☐ Better ways to overcome resistance to change

☐ Improved communication and work relationships

☐ Enhanced commitment, engagement, and motivation

☐ Increased flexibility

☐ Decreased conflict and dissatisfaction

☐ More positive attitudes

☐ Less complaining

☐ More productive problem solving

☐ More creativity and innovation from diverse perspectives

☐ More openness, honesty, and trust

☐ Decreased turnover

☐ Reduced time wasted on non-productive activity

☐ Fewer hidden agendas

acknowledge to yourself that your feeling response is your body's warning system signaling to you that something important to you has happened. This acknowledgment gives you information to understand yourself better. Knowing that is a first step in dealing with the situation. However, acknowledging feelings may be challenging because most of us were taught to disregard or disengage this warning system. Think of the early messages you were given that taught you to ignore your feelings. When you demonstrated an emotion, you may have heard messages such as these:

- Now, just calm down.

- Don't get so upset.

- Chill out.

- Big boys don't cry.

- Be a big girl.

- Don't be such a drama queen.

- Keep a stiff upper lip.

- Just relax.

- Cut out the dramatics.

Not only do these messages tell you to suppress your emotions, they often lead you to be ashamed of having them so that you don't even want to admit them to yourself.

We Can't Hide Emotions

Even if you think you can keep them hidden, your feelings show. The clenched jaw, flared nostrils, blushing skin, wide eyes, sullen silence, breaking voice, nervous cough, or rapid speech give you away. Poker faces are rare because others can usually read your feelings before you are consciously aware of them. Sometimes you may fool yourself into thinking you are hiding them or you confuse people by sending mixed signals, saying, "No, I'm not angry," when you are enraged, or, "That's fine with me," when you are not in agreement at all.

Emotions Are at Work Whether We Acknowledge Them or Not

When you ignore or deny your feelings, you allow them to work without any direction. Like wind or water, emotions are an unharnessed source of energy that operates, influencing situations and directing your behavior. Once you become aware of what your feelings are and how they are affecting you, you have choices about how to manage them. However, if you don't admit them, they do their work anyway. They get dealt with one way or another.

We saw this factor being addressed recently in an unexpected way. A group of stockbrokers shared a retreat facility with us during an emotional intelligence and diversity training program. We were surprised to learn that the topic of their session was also emotional intelligence. They told us they recognized that while in their work they were supposed to be rational and objective, emotions played a powerful role in their decisions and those of their clients. They had requested this training session to learn how to understand and use the important information that feelings brought to the decision process and to gain ways to manage their emotions so they did not negatively cloud the process.

All Interactions Have Both Rational and Emotional Elements

Conversations, relationships, and interpersonal interactions are like sheet music, with both lyrics and a melody. The rational element is much like the words of a song that carries the stated message. The emotional aspect is like the tune that supports the words. Think about some of your interactions and see if you can find both parts—the words and the feelings, both the rational aspect, the facts, and the emotional part, the feelings.

- You get a gift from an employee. That's the rational part. You are uncomfortable because it feels like a bribe, or you feel touched at your staff member's thoughtfulness. That's the feeling aspect.

- You are asked to head an important task force. That's the rational part. You feel complimented to be given such an honor, or you feel anxious, as though you've been set up to fail. That's the feeling aspect.

- You give an employee a semiannual performance review. That's the rational part. The employee feels valued and appreciates the suggestions you've given for development, or feels put down and discriminated against by your feedback. That's the feeling aspect.

As you can see from these examples, there is often more than one possible feeling response to a situation, and being able to manage that choice is key. There is an interaction between thoughts and emotions that produces consequences, and part of emotional intelligence is taking charge of the thinking that leads to feelings.

Addressing Underlying Feelings to Resolve Difficult Situations and Conflicts

All the suggestions and solutions in the world won't fix a relationship problem unless the emotional aspect is addressed, because the feelings, if not dealt with, will continue to undermine any attempt at resolution. As the title of John Gray's book so aptly says, *What You Can Feel You Can Heal;* conversely, it's hard to heal what you can't or won't admit you feel. Until you feel that your boss has your best interests at heart, you'll have a hard time using her feedback. Unless your employee feels you are being honest, he won't follow your lead. Until you acknowledge your discomfort with a particular group, you won't be able to deal well with people of that group. Unless your co-worker feels safe enough to disclose her fear, you won't be able to understand her reluctance about making presentations. Only when your colleague trusts your motives will he be willing to help you out.

Steps to Capturing and Using the Energy of Emotions

Ask yourself the following questions as a start toward capturing and using your emotional energy:

- What is this feeling reaction telling me about what matters to me?
- What are my body's signs that show my feelings? What signs do I see in others?
- How are my feelings influencing my life and my behavior?
- What are both the rational and emotional elements of this interaction?
- What feelings are operating in this situation—mine and others'?

Gaining Fluency in the Vocabulary of Emotions

A key step in capturing the power of feelings is becoming fluent in the vocabulary of emotions. Most people have a limited lexicon when it comes to emotions. Humans don't come into this world with labels for feelings. Babies simply experience physical sensations such as hunger, pain, or being wet. As they grow and develop, they are given names for what they are experiencing by parents and others. For example:

- You hit your sister because you were *jealous* that she got so many presents for her birthday.

- You are crying because you are *embarrassed* that you had an accident and wet your pants.

- You are *angry* because Mommy won't buy you the toy you want at the checkout counter.

Little by little through these kinds of messages, individuals develop language for their emotional responses. When we give seminar participants three minutes to write as many feelings as they can, they usually run out of steam after listing the most common ones: anger, irritation, happiness, love, pressure, joy, fear, tension, upset, frustration, depression, and worry.

However, you experience a much wider range of feelings with important nuances, and the first step in becoming emotionally intelligent is to be able to articulate the feelings you are experiencing. It is different to feel inadequate rather than depressed, rejected rather than disrespected, sad rather than anxious over a loss. When you can identify and label your feelings, you are stronger and better prepared to deal with them. This increases your self-esteem, sense of control, and ability to manage your world. See if you can list ten emotions you've experienced during the past week at work. (If you need help, take a look at the list of feelings, or "Vocabulary of Emotions," in Chapter 3.) Think about your reactions and behaviors when you experienced those emotions. Also think about the emotions you have observed in others with whom you work and how you responded to their feelings.

If you would like to be more in charge of those reactions and how you respond, the rest of this book is your ally, because it gives you the know-how to

---

Figure 1

Steps Toward Emotional Intelligence

1. *Identify* the feelings you are experiencing.

Cultivate a vocabulary of emotions so you can accurately identify what you are feeling. Are you frustrated or confused, hurt or angry, overwhelmed or lacking confidence? Being able to admit and name the feeling is the first step.

2. *Understand* your feeling response.

Look inside to find out what is going on for you. Why are you reacting this way? What is this feeling response telling you? Where did this reaction come from? Digging inside to gain a deeper understanding of yourself will enable you to predict your own reactions.

3. *Manage* your emotional response.

Once you know and understand the feeling, you need to deal with it. It is at this point that you recognize your options and choose the best one in the situation. Should you confront, and if so, how? Should you do more investigating before you respond? Do you need a cooling-off period? What do you want out of this situation, and what is the best way to get it? This is the step that ensures that you are in charge of your emotions rather than having your emotions direct you.

4. *Communicate* your feelings and needs to others.

Letting others know how you feel is critical, and you cannot behave with emotional intelligence without communicating your feelings effectively. Communication helps eliminate the confusion and mixed messages that are all too common and helps build trust and openness through transparency.

5. *Apply* the power of emotions in your relationships.

Using what you know about your feelings and the feelings of others in a productive way is the final step in making sure you are not just right but effective.

---

do that. *Emotional intelligence* is the ability to access and understand feelings and use their energy in productive ways. Beyond understanding, it involves specific actions in recognizing feelings, understanding them, articulating them, and then applying their power effectively. Emotions are not too soft to deal with. You can learn specific skills that are involved in emotional intelligence and take five concrete steps, shown in Figure 1, that will allow you to behave in powerful and healthy ways to be not just right but effective.

The Next Steps

The next four chapters of this book will give you the tools and methods to develop these abilities through the four aspects, or dimensions, of emotional intelligence and diversity:

- Affirmative Introspection
- Self-Governance
- Intercultural Literacy
- Social Architecting

These tools can help you understand and develop your emotional intelligence and apply the power of that intelligence effectively.

2

We "Can't All Just Get Along"

One of the legacies of the March 1991 beating of Rodney King by four officers of the Los Angeles Police Department, and the subsequent Los Angeles riots in April 1992 after the King verdict, was Rodney's simple phrase, more statement than question: "Can't we all just get along?" The entire Rodney King incident is a memorable and relevant example of what happens when human beings lose control of their emotions, of feelings being out of control and destructive.

The Emotional Intelligence and Diversity (EID) Model is unique and different from the general understanding of emotional intelligence. The model is designed to help those who work together in organizations learn how to manage emotions in healthy, productive ways at times when differences might trigger the worst and most volatile reactions. Not only a tool for personal use, the model is a framework for human resources professionals, diversity officers, organization development and training specialists, and managers to use to guide staff members. This outcome is critical not only for you but also for those whom you manage and those with whom you work. We will explain the EID Model, but first we discuss how and why differences trigger our emotions.

The Safety Factor

All human beings want and need to feel safe and secure in their world. Whether you are a manager leading an important meeting where key issues have to be resolved amid expected conflict or you are tired and merely trying to get home safely at the end of a long workday, as a human being you like predictability. You set up your world, like that of others, so that you feel safe and secure. Those feelings of safety and security are enhanced when you create worlds with people who are like you. You can be like or unlike others in many different ways, starting with the obvious: gender, skin color, and age. But many of the differences that spark volatile emotions are unrelated to the visible differences. Just look at a few issues in today's world that can trigger potent feelings.

- Inclusion or exclusion of religion in public life

- Pro-life or pro-choice views

- Conservative or liberal political views

- A monolingual or a multilingual workplace

- Amnesty for immigrants or sending undocumented people back to their home countries

- Organization-specific policies, procedures, and priorities at work over which employees have different viewpoints

If you have had conversations with people across a spectrum of beliefs on these kinds of issues, you know what we mean. Maybe you even have strong emotional reactions to some of these issues. The goal of the EID Model is to give you the skills and tools to deal with these differences in an open, safe way so that real dialogue can take place, leading to solutions that work for all. This book is about helping you be less fearful of differences and more confident in bringing them to an effective conclusion. But first, the next section discusses how people deal with differences, an important starting point that will help you as you begin gaining tools and skills.

Control and Approval Needs

Critical to enhancing feelings of safety, your needs for control and approval are in some ways subtle and primal, and in other ways obvious. They are foundational to perceptions of safety. People who feel out of control in their lives, or who do not feel approval and regard from themselves and others, have no safety platform on which to stand. When they don't feel that basic safety, they have difficulty dealing with differences in an emotionally healthy way. Control and approval needs underlie the psychological health of the human species. Stated simply, human beings need the following:

- To control their world

- To have approval from self and others

Dealing with differences often challenges your ability to meet these needs. Whether you are age three, twenty-three, forty-three, or sixty-three, those same two needs exist. At three, you may be trying to navigate your way around all the nooks and crannies of your house (control) and get the experience of seeing Mom and Dad's awe (approval) at your cleverness and agility. At twenty-three, you have finished school, are starting a new job, and are deciding where to live. At forty-three, you are seeking satisfaction at work along with that promotion you want. At sixty-three, you are contemplating retirement as you structure a life of satisfaction, adventure, peacefulness. Whatever control and approval look like to you, you spend a lifetime striving for them. Your choices in life don't come labeled control and approval, but they are at the base of your emotional health, and your reactions are linked to getting those two needs met.

Think about what the implications of control and approval are for you as a manager. Think back on those individuals you have managed. Most managers can remember employees who dynamite good feelings in a work group, those who enter a room and change the chemistry in a negative way. Trying to coach a change in a situation like that is not easy. Virtually all managers have experienced dissonant chemistry. Sometimes the employee's awareness level is low, but you do know that this person is alive and in your space—and that is bad. When you think back to those situations or people, look at your own patterns. Your feelings and the ability to be effective may be more susceptible to control feelings than to approval or vice versa. At this point, just reflect, identify particular situations where control and approval implications surfaced, and think about the impact on your effectiveness as a manager. The best way to loosen the grip of these influences on your reactions is to be aware and plan around them. Ask yourself: how does this situation challenge my control and/or approval needs?

Increased Openness or Less Judgmentalness

How you deal with different ideas, preferences, and practices also influences feelings of safety. Baskin-Robbins, with its famous thirty-one flavors of ice cream, provides a metaphor to make the point that different views and opinions are simply that—different. Few things in life are actually right or wrong. While all humans like some things better than others, few of those things are inherently better or worse. Some days that reality is easier to remember than others. To the degree that you can actually see the world this way and convey that in your work, you will project openness and not be threatened by different views. That openness will serve you well as a manager. Ask yourself: what is the upside and downside of this situation or viewpoint?

Less Rigid or More Fluid Expectations

When we mention flexibility as a way to create more openness and less fear or threat of differences, managers often get nervous. They worry that they will appear weak and indecisive, that they will have to lower standards. They are concerned that their people won't come through. They fear that fluid expectations will lead to underachievement and a negative reflection of the manager's group (control and approval issues anyone?). Seeing expectations as a starting point rather than a fixed point is an easy and miraculous way to begin practicing.

The Four Layers of Diversity: Reflecting on the Differences That Trigger Emotions

This chapter began with a discussion about why, and how powerfully, emotions can be kicked up amid differences with some look at the potential consequences. It also talked, in a general sense, about the human species and its feelings of threat or fear in the face of differences. This section will focus on these differences relating to you as a manager in the workplace. The Four Layers of Diversity Model (in Figure 2) is the starting point for a conversation about different perspectives and different realities. The end point is about how these differences can enhance you, a work group, and an organization in a rich and satisfying way.

Figure 2: Four Layers of Diversity

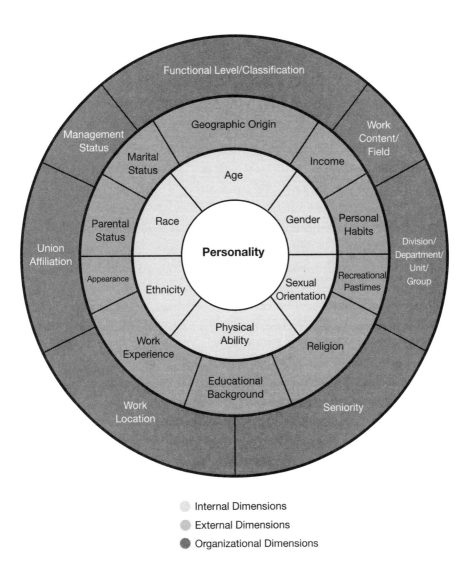

Sources: Adapted with permission from Lee Gardenswartz and Anita Rowe, *Diverse Teams at Work* (Alexandria, VA: Society for Human Resource Management, 2003), 33. The concepts of internal dimensions and external dimensions are adapted from Marilyn Loden and Judy Rosener, *Workforce America!* (Homewood, IL: Business One Irwin, 1991).

Having worked in the field loosely labeled diversity for the past thirty years, we remember the early days when positive comments about diversity were scarce. At the time the best many groups could say about the increasing differences in their communities in the United States was that the new ethnic restaurant in the neighborhood served tasty cuisine. We even remember the man who, in the middle of one of our lectures on demographic changes, walked out, taking his clenched jaw and his scowling face with him. We imagine that his fear of dealing with what appeared to be monumental differences overwhelmed him. The quickest and most obvious judgments about others generally focus on similarities and differences on the basis of external appearance, but those are not always the points of connection or disconnection that matter most once we get past the obvious.

You can use the Four Layers of Diversity Model not only to dissect and understand the complexity you face today but also to look in the mirror and see what differences actually bother or irritate you and those who report to you. Sometimes those differences between co-workers can be the source of one another's biggest irritants.

Personality: Everyone Has One

As obvious as it seems, participants in workshops today still nod in both agreement and shock that they didn't see this one sooner. Personality matters. It is a huge diversity issue. All relationships don't work equally well, and there is no accounting for interpersonal chemistry or lack of it. Some people rub you the right way, and some, the wrong. When someone you like has a belief, value, habit, or priority that differs from yours, you will often find it easier to consider its merits than if it came from someone you didn't like.

There are certain qualities, beliefs, characteristics, styles and values that you are positively predisposed toward. There are others you are not. If you are like most people, patience and understanding, or even appreciation, for these differences is not equal. A greeting card by Irving Becker expresses a simple but profound truth with huge implications for the personality aspect of dealing with diversity: "If you don't like someone, the way he holds his spoon will make you furious; if you do like him, he can turn his plate over into your lap and you won't mind."

So much for being objective. You are human: you have personality preferences, and you have personality dislikes. To be a supremely effective manager, you can start by identifying your biases, both pro and con. Look at the list in Activity 1. See which qualities are must-haves for those who report to you, which ones are desirable, and finally which ones set you on edge and make dealing with differences difficult.

Activity 1

Identifying Personality Trait Preferences

As a manager, which traits do you demand? Which do you want or prefer? And which do you flat out dislike? Think about what happens to you when you get something other than what you want.

	Demand	Want	Dislike
Always on time; focused			
Relaxed, flexible approach to time			
A problem solver; positive attitude			
Good at taking direction, not at taking initiative			
Sees the hierarchy and goes around it to get things done			
Sees the hierarchy and honors it			
Likes to talk with and connect to others in the group			
Sees the workplace as a place for doing a job; privacy is important			
Always looks forward; wants to change things			
Always looks back; honors tradition			

Activity 1 (continued)

	Demand	Want	Dislike
Introverted and prefers to work alone			
Extroverted, gregarious			
Goes by the book			
Throws the book out			

These are just some of the many examples of personality traits you will find on your team. Look in that mirror. Be honest. Which ones produced a strong reaction? Do yourself a favor. Keep a log and start noticing, then record a few of your reactions, both when things are very positive and when your reactions are anything but.

- I reacted strongly to the following examples:

  Positive behavior _____

  Negative behavior _____

- Other behaviors that I really like and want are _____

  _____

  The ones that trigger negative emotions are _____

  _____

- The clues that indicate my negative emotions have been triggered are:

  _____

  _____

Internal Dimensions: The Potential for Judging a Book by Its Cover

The internal dimensions are the ones most people associate with diversity, because these are the protected categories. Violate human and civil rights here, and you or your organization can end up in court and in deep financial trouble. As you read examples of how some of these differences trigger emotions in the workplace, see which ones you have experienced.

Age

People today seem to have the shortest emotional fuse over age differences in the workplace. Frustration and misjudgments about age-related stereotypes are everywhere, and they include the following ones about people in their sixties:

- The person has retired on the job.
- The person has no new ideas and no imagination.
- The person is not tech savvy, or even literate, and maybe technophobic.
- The person is slow to think, move, and act.
- The person is unwilling to be open to new ways of doing things.

They also include the following ones about people in their twenties:

- The person wants everything right now.
- The person doesn't want to pay dues or do what it takes to earn promotion.
- The person is so busy multitasking and text messaging that it's hard to see the employee focus and get any work done.
- The person has no loyalty.

What seems to push the generational buttons of people across the age spectrum is a perception of being devalued, misunderstood, and not respected. As a manager, you can have a profound impact on helping your group see the incredible value that different ages can provide and on creating an environment of mutual respect.

Gender

We have seen definite progress in dealing with differences in gender. Nevertheless, in some organizations, particularly in uniformed services like police and fire departments, we see ample room for growth. As a rule, blatant discrimination is less present today than in the past. Whereas women used to have a hard time getting accepted to medical or law school, they now often make up 50 percent or more of the class. Some of the most mean-spirited conflicts occur between women who work and women who stay at home to raise children. There can be a painful lack of respect on both sides, and we suspect control and approval issues are again at work here.

As you look in the mirror for any gender buttons that get pushed, ask yourself the following:

- Do you ever use a gender label to describe someone in a role, such as a male nurse or a female financial analyst? If so, there is work to do.

- Do you always consider a wide array of candidates for opportunities, promotions, and special projects, especially ones that will break the gender stereotypes?

- When was the last time gender was important in your reaction to someone? You might have experienced anything from confusion about how to respond, to delayed anger at a perceived slight, to surprise at an unconscious stereotype. What was that about?

Sexual orientation

This dimension still results in the most overt resistance and discomfort in training session discussions. For starters, all human beings have a sexual orientation and fit somewhere on this continuum:

Demonstrations of sexual behavior have no place in the work environment for anyone, heterosexual or gay and lesbian. In dealing with this dimension in an emotionally intelligent way, can each person be who he or she is, or does a person have to hide? People can put pictures of spouses, kids, cats, and dogs on their desk. If someone is gay or lesbian, can that person put a picture of his or her partner in a picture frame for all to see? That's the acid test.

When you look in the mirror, what do you see about your own reactions?

- Will people who report to you tell you if their sexual orientation is different from that of most co-workers?

- What are the bounds of your tolerance and what, if anything, pushes you away from the topic or people whose sexual orientation is different from yours?

- When you feel uncomfortable, what is your emotional response? How is that shown in your behavior?

These are important questions to think about, as are your responses. If you say that you don't know anyone who is gay or lesbian, you might start by challenging that thought. Perhaps people are afraid to tell you.

Physical ability

As a manager, you are in charge of a group with different physical abilities. Sometimes, you deal with the obvious physical ability issues, such as someone who uses a hearing aid, crutches, or a wheelchair. Sometimes, physical ability presents itself as an opportunity, such as when someone has the strength or size to help get a job done. Talked about infrequently are the less visible physical issues: people who can't see well but aren't blind; people who can't hear well but don't have a hearing aid; or people whose knees are swollen and giving them pain, but they have no crutches. Not all physical ability issues are obvious.

From an emotional intelligence and diversity standpoint, the obvious disabilities are most important because they tend to generate discomfort in others. People aren't sure what the boundaries are. What can they ask? Should they offer to help? What is the definition of being insensitive and going too far? There may be other feelings as well, but discomfort for able-bodied people who feel uneasy about asking questions is real. Sometimes discomfort can also arise for the person with a physical disability who feels that he or she makes extra work for others.

As the manager, you can model grace and sensitivity by building real connections with everyone so that when you do ask questions, they will be taken not only in the right way but, more importantly, in the context of a respectful relationship.

When you look in the mirror, what do you see?

- Where are your own areas of discomfort?

- When do you avoid the subject of physical ability issues?

- When you do avoid the subject, what are the consequences?

- What is one way to increase your comfort in this area?

- What can you do in your role as manager to help others feel more comfortable in this area?

Ethnicity

Ethnicity is the place to assess, own, and acknowledge your ancestral heritage. Everyone has ancestors and as a result eats certain foods, observes certain holidays, and speaks one, two, or multiple languages. This can become a volatile area because of language differences in the workplace, and even because of debate around immigration policy. It has been, and still can be, a divisive issue.

If you manage people from different parts of the world, whether there is an intact team you see daily or a virtual team you see face to face rarely, one of your biggest jobs as a manager will be to create openness and respect for differences. Ask yourself these questions in the mirror.

- Where do your hot buttons get pushed around ethnicity?

- What conflicts seem to appear because of differences or misunderstandings around cultural differences related to ethnicity?

- Whose feelings must you deal with around ethnic differences on your team, and what are the issues?

Race

This dimension of diversity has two coexisting truths. Thankfully, a lot of progress has been made in the United States, especially since the 1960s. We do not want to deny the very real and specific gains. Having acknowledged those, we must also own the fact that there is also a distance still to travel. Race is still an issue in many organizations and communities, and the country has a history infused with bitterness, hurt, violence, pain, and injustice, so it is difficult when dealing with race to have people leave their anxiety at home. The concept of race involves observable physical characteristics such as skin color, eye shape, hair texture, and bone structure.

Does race still matter? You decide after reading about one person's experience. We were talking about race in a session when an African American participant from North Carolina told us a story, one that he believed all black people would relate to but one that would surprise the whites in the room. He was trying to sell his house in a nice neighborhood, and other houses were moving but not his. His real estate agent finally made a suggestion, one that she regretted but one that she thought might make the house sell more quickly. Her suggestion? Take down all the family pictures that showed him and his African American family and put them away for a bit. The house sold immediately. We would like to say that this is one person's story, an aberration, but every black person in our class nodded in an "of course that's how it is" fashion. White participants gasped. Race still matters. The question for you as a manager is, what feelings are triggered in you because of it?

- Are you afraid to give an employee of a different race a bad review because he'll claim discrimination?

- Do you worry about how the cultural norms and behaviors of different racial groups are affecting team dynamics?

- If there are conflicts on the team due to racial differences, are you comfortable dealing with them and trying to build bridges?

- Where do your own inadequacies surface, and what emotions come to the surface when you feel unsure about how to deal with situations involving race?

External Dimensions: Everyone Is a Composite of Many Forces, Factors, and Influences

The third layer of the diversity model involves aspects of people's identities that are also important and undoubtedly influence you directly and indirectly as a manager. However, unlike age, gender, and the other internal dimensions, which are not changeable, those aspects of people in the external dimensions do have the capacity to be altered. People can get married or divorced. They can go back to school to get more education or take up a new hobby. They may even expand their religious practices and beliefs or decide to opt out of religion. Look these over and see which are most important in your work group. Among the most common influences in that layer are the following, with examples of potential relevance for you in a management role.

Geographic origin

People were all raised somewhere, and some people grew up in several or many different places. Where you grow up (in the United States or outside of it, in a rural or urban area, in which geographic region within the United States) profoundly influences who you are and how you view the world. This influence is absorbed by osmosis, and you don't even realize the fingerprints until you go elsewhere. As a manager, if you know this about people, you will go a long way toward building both relationships and understanding.

- What do you already know about where your employees were reared?

- How does it influence them?

- If you don't know, how will you find out?

The external dimensions are strongly influential, and because this model is fluid, you may see external dimensions in your employees that are important but missing from our model. That's no problem. Just factor them in.

Income

Socioeconomics is frequently an issue and is often discussed in terms of class. It is an infrequently mentioned but very real issue in diversity. We actually think that is the "dirty little secret" people don't talk much about in the United States, but it is huge. Poverty, or being in the low socioeconomic level, makes visible differences more obvious and relevant. On the other hand, affluence seems to be a nice connector across racial and ethnic divides. When people have little financially and struggle to make ends meet, the differences in the internal dimensions are exacerbated. Think about how it plays out in your organization.

- Does a person's income influence how he or she dresses? Does it influence who the person socializes with or recreates with in the group? Golf is expensive. Whom does that limit?

- Does lack of money present an invisible but certain barrier to upward mobility? Cite an example if you think it does.

- How does income, or lack of it, shape the subtle expectations and opportunities you either see or don't see for people you manage?

Recreational pastimes

The recreational pastime of choice in corporate America is golf, but depending on geography, industry, and socioeconomics, other pastimes such as fishing, hiking, bowling, or even theater or crafts can be part of how people socialize. The importance of recreational pastimes is that bonds are built in an informal atmosphere, and camaraderie develops. There are important opportunities to build cohesion and respect through recreation. Think about the role of recreation in your group.

- How many different ways do people like to enjoy themselves in their leisure?

- If you don't know this information, how will you find out?

- How will you help all employees expand their repertoire?

Creating relationships in informal settings builds connection and understanding in the workplace and, as a result, can soften some of the emotional rough edges when differences surface.

Educational background

Your impact can be huge in helping people across the educational divide develop mutual respect and appreciation. There are not only approval issues tied to educational background but control issues as well. Many career opportunity doors close without degrees.

- Do people have degrees?

- From where? Does it matter what college or university a degree is from, or is any sheepskin acceptable?

- What about the stellar performer who has no degree but who has learned on the job and teaches co-workers all the time in ways big and small. What chances does this person have to get promoted?

- How do you see yourself? Are you a roadblock? An encourager? A coach?

Appearance

Appearance matters: studies show how quickly people size other people up and judge them based on what they see. They judge a person based on aspects such as height, weight, skin color, hair style, clothes, and piercings and tattoos, all of which can determine the trajectory of a person's career opportunities. Doors can be both opened and closed because of a person's appearance. A manager has a heavy responsibility to get beyond appearance, a responsibility that presents opportunities for self-growth and the chance to help others get beyond appearance as well.

- When do you see people dismissed or discounted because of appearance?

- What dimensions of appearance really do and should matter? Which are irrelevant?

- What fatal mistakes in appearance are made in your organization or on your team?

- How can you help people grow beyond the stereotypes?

Parental status

Parental status has been a central issue over the years in our clients' organizations because employees love both their children and their work, and they seek a balance between the two. When employees don't have balance, when life tilts more toward work, frustration can result.

- How do you manage your workplace so that the work gets done while also acknowledging and allowing for some flexibility so people can honor their commitments to both work and family?

- How does the child or no child issue surface? Is there a sense that those who don't have kids pick up extra work for those who do? If so, what emotions or resentments are triggered? How can you create a workplace that respects both realities?

Marital status

We have seen differences in how people spend after-hours time together and what the expectations are. If employees are single, there may be more discretionary time to socialize after work. When people have families, they often feel constrained after hours and interact less with co-workers. How might these realities or others around marital status impact the dynamics of your team?

Organizational Dimensions: Opportunities for Inclusion and Exclusion

The last layer of the diversity model is about the organization itself. It takes into account the following:

- Functional level or classification in the organization
- Work content or field of work
- Department, division, unit, and work group
- Length of service or seniority
- Work location
- Union and management differences (where applicable)
- Management status

As a manager, you may not be able to control decisions and policies for the whole organization systemwide, but you are the strongest factor in people's connection to the organization. This is a large responsibility and requires asking some important questions. Your answers will go a long way toward determining how your employees view differences and how they handle them when they occur. Your answers will also influence whether they just cope and tolerate differences or really relish and leverage them.

- What can you do to create a safe environment in which differences are valued and appreciated?
- How do you provide a role model for dealing with differences respectfully when they are present?
- More to the point, how do you show that you need, relish, and expect differences?
- What is the most important message you can send to those you manage about dealing with their emotions in a world of difference?

The Four Layers of Diversity explanation serves as a backdrop to introduce some of the many differences you are faced with as a manager, differences that may trigger emotional responses. Handling your emotions effectively is critical. Being a role model, coach, and teacher to your employees is just as critical. An introduction to the EID Model will help you gain insight about the tools and skills this book will help you develop.

The Four Parts of Dealing with Emotions in a Diverse World

We three authors of this book, Jorge, Lee, and Anita, probably have close to seventy-five years of experience among us in teaching others how to deal with diversity, and we created this model out of that experience. In the process of doing his counseling and teaching at UCLA, Jorge thought that an emotional intelligence and diversity connection had something to offer participants in our training sessions because his emotional intelligence classes were always full. As the three of us talked, we realized that the missing piece or "what's next" question could be answered by looking at how emotional intelligence helps people deal with all the differences that they encounter in the process of living life every day. Surely, just the speed of change and the pervasiveness of technology bring differences that trigger emotions. Add to that the effects of changing demographics and globalization in every part of life, and it is clear that emotions, whether coping with differences in the local community or around the world, provide ample opportunity for people to practice their emotional intelligence.

The emotional intelligence you need to deal with diversity includes both insight and action, both knowing and doing. One is not enough without the other. And you need to focus on yourself and others. The four parts of EID about which you will develop an understanding as you read this book are shown in the model in Figure 3.

Affirmative Introspection helps you gain insight about yourself. *Self-Governance* focuses on managing yourself and your reactions. *Intercultural Literacy* helps you understand others. *Social Architecting* shows you how to manage your interactions with others and the environments you share with them.

Figure 3: Emotional Intelligence and Diversity Model

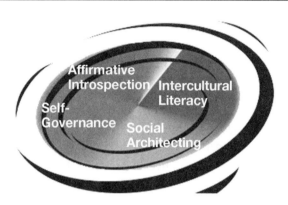

Each part of the model will be explored in more depth throughout the book, but this section gives an overview of the model as a whole and of each part as a mirror for your insight or awareness and a map for your action.

Affirmative Introspection—Taking a Look Inside

Dealing with diversity is an inside job. It is not about getting lists of behaviors for how to deal with other people, whether those people are executives or union stewards or are of Chinese or British origin. Rather it is about looking inside yourself and becoming aware of your feelings and reactions, your behaviors and beliefs, and how you respond to others when their values, beliefs, and priorities differ from yours. The concept of Affirmative Introspection is about acknowledging, owning, and accepting who you are—the good, the bad, the beautiful, the ugly.

This introspection does not seem to be easy for most individuals. Over the years, when we have asked people to honestly proclaim their strengths, as well as areas that provide opportunity for growth, they were always reluctant to claim strengths, fearing that they would come across as arrogant. To make matters worse, they would beat themselves up for the qualities they were missing but needed and wanted. The mirror, which Affirmative Introspection invokes, asks you as a person and a manager to look at your reflection without harsh judgment. Just accept the person in the mirror. Where you have strengths, own them. It is not boastful to understand yourself and use your strengths for your good and the good of others.

Furthermore, you may have also noticed that all human beings are flawed and fall short. Where are you lacking as a manager? Think seriously about where you could improve. This does not mean you are deficient or unworthy; it means you are human and can improve. The essence of Affirmative Introspection is dispassionate self-acceptance that acknowledges equally your strengths and your areas for improvement. You then go about the business of improving. As a manager, showing people how to deal with their emotions while also being proportional about the parts of themselves they admire and those they don't is a worthy management and coaching goal that will yield positive results.

The three skills in Affirmative Introspection are the following:

- Knowing what makes you tick

- Being comfortable in your own skin

- Being aware of your own biases and hot buttons

Knowing what makes you tick

There is no substitute for self-awareness. Socrates said, "Know thyself." If you know yourself, you know what your habits and patterns are with those you manage. You can gauge which reactions work and which do not, and when necessary you can adjust and do things differently. But to change your reactions, you first have to know what makes you tick.

Being comfortable in your own skin

Being comfortable with who you are, no matter where you are, is a critical leadership and management skill. There is no substitute for self-comfort because it conveys an internal safety net that makes you much less threatened by differences. When you are comfortable with who you are, you convey that others are also safe being who they are. This safety and acceptance means that you are not reacting negatively to differences and that others don't need to react negatively either. There is a way of using the differences for good, not reacting out of disgust, disapproval, or fear.

Being aware of your own biases and hot buttons

When you know yourself well and accept yourself as you are, you also acknowledge that there are things that bother you. You aren't a robot—you do have feelings about people, experiences, values, and beliefs, and sometimes your emotions get triggered. It really helps you as a manager to know that when Mary is late to a meeting again you might react because you interpret her lateness as disrespectful. When Luis makes decisions without seeking input, you also react because you want ownership and engagement. Knowing your habitual response gets you ready for the map in the next section, on Self-Governance.

Self-Governance—Getting a Handle on Your Feelings

Self-Governance, the second aspect of the EID Model, is a map, because it gives you a road to travel for taking action to deal with the range and intensity of emotions triggered by differences. Self-Governance is not about controlling emotions. Rather, it is about managing them. Neither spewing emotions, acting like a volcano that erupts, nor suppressing emotions, like an earthquake that rumbles and causes havoc when too much activity is buried underground, is a good way to handle feelings. The energy of emotions needs to be managed and channeled in a constructive way. Self-Governance offers three precise and healthy ways to manage feelings.

The three skills in Self-Governance are the following:

- Making ambiguity an ally

- Becoming a change master

- Getting in charge of your self-talk

Making ambiguity an ally

This is one of the most important concepts in EID. What it says is that life, especially in the diverse workplace, is complex and very few things are truly right or wrong. Dilemmas come when you have a right choice versus another right choice, or an undesirable choice versus another undesirable choice. Making ambiguity an ally suggests that as a manager, judgment is key, and clear rights and clear wrongs are few and far between. Helping others wrestle with complexity and nuance is an appropriate and necessary skill in today's world and a way to help co-workers manage their feelings in the process.

Becoming a change master

Human beings are experiencing rapid change as never before in human history. When you realize that as a species human beings like homeostasis and predictability, you really grasp that emotional reserves get severely tested in the beginning of the twenty-first century. But those species that don't adapt die. Being fluid with our emotional responses and accepting change as a given are starting points. Fifteen years ago we helped a telephone company deal with change by conducting forty managing change seminars so staff could really come to grips with change. It was wrenching. Expectations of the company held by employees based on prior history could no longer be met. It was an extraordinarily difficult adjustment for employees to make. Some made it, and some didn't. Those that didn't told us they made a conscious choice to hang on to their anger. They felt righteous, and that bolstered them. Long-term, that anger and resentment from not adapting costs your body and your effectiveness in all parts of your life. As a manager, it also sets a terrible example.

Getting in charge of your self-talk

If there is one book that basically states "you are what you think," there must be thousands. It is difficult to pick up a book in the psychology section of a bookstore that does not talk about the importance of attitudes and the messages you tell yourself. The late Albert Ellis made a huge contribution to this field with his creation of Rational Emotive Therapy. We have never met a person who talked about how awful life is who ended up feeling better after that internal conversation. Nor have we met a person who had a more positive impact on others because of the harmful, negative messages he told himself. One clear destination on your road map toward change is using more realistic, helpful internal messages.

Intercultural Literacy—Reading Others Accurately

Focusing on yourself is only half the job in dealing with differences. Understanding others and, as a manager, getting the best from them, are the other parts of the equation. This involves knowledge about cultural differences that influence our behavior. Defined by Geert Hofstede as "behavioral software," culture is the set of rules, norms, and preferences that tell us how to behave and how to interpret the behavior of others. Hofstede's work focuses primarily on the range of cultural differences across civilizations (East and West) and borders by looking at countries around the world. His software metaphor could, however, be applied to cultures that exist within family structures, departments in organizations, or anywhere people congregate to operate together for some purpose. Certainly within a corporation, no one would expect departments as different as technology, tax and accounting, sales, or human resources to have the same culture. The norms of each department derive from those who are a part of it and from their definition of who they are and why they exist.

The three skills in Intercultural Literacy are the following:

- Understanding the cultural whys behind behavior

- Seeing the upsides and downsides of all cultural norms

- Transcending your own perspective and showing empathy

Understanding the cultural whys behind behavior

Understanding cultural whys behind behavior helps people recognize a wide array of norms that exist around the world, from how people communicate (e.g., directly or circuitously) to how they participate in meetings, greet each other, or decide how close or far to stand from one another. These differences certainly exist around the globe. Close to home we suggest that they exist in family structures. Take a look at siblings raised in the same home when they grow up and make their way in the world. The manager who can help others develop awareness, knowledge, and understanding will also create acceptance and patience, two very necessary qualities for dealing well with differences.

Seeing the upsides and downsides of all cultural norms

Here our mirror metaphor is clear and sharp. You look in the mirror, and to the degree that the reflection that comes back looks similar to you, that's the degree to which you feel comfort and acceptance. It is part of the human species to seek likeness. There is nothing wrong with desiring it or seeking it out. What blunts your emotional intelligence in a diverse world is when you judge people's norms that are different from yours as inferior to yours. Here's an example. For a person reared in the United States, it would be difficult to not absorb the culture of individualism. "It's a free country, and I can do my own thing" is an example of this. Over time, that belief begins to feel comfortable and becomes a part of how you see the world. Individualism certainly has its merits. It is crucial in developing creativity and initiative. It allows people to venture forth on their own and take risks. It encourages autonomy and achievement. But it has downsides. It can feel selfish and isolating. It lacks esprit de corps, and often group productivity is better than what any one person can do on his or her own. Likewise, being from a collectivist culture also has strengths and drawbacks. Being able to objectively see the benefits and limits of all norms goes a long way toward helping people deal more effectively with their feelings around differences, and this is a strategy any manager can teach, utilize, and reinforce.

Transcending your own perspective and showing empathy

Empathy is one of the truly critical skills in becoming an effective manager and human being, especially when it comes to bridging differences. At its most basic, empathy is the ability to identify a person's feelings or emotional state and accept that person's right to feel the way he does. It does not mean you agree with his feelings. What it does mean is that you connect at the most fundamental level, because you understand where a person is in her life at some moment and you accept and acknowledge her right to be there. If you have had a similar experience in life and you can genuinely relate, that is a bonus. Simply stated, as a manager and a person, identifying someone's feelings, relating when you can based on your experience, and, finally, accepting a person's right to feel that way is what empathy is about. That's all. The manager who has the know-how and who also takes the time to be empathetic will inspire incredible loyalty and commitment.

Social Architecting—Enrolling and Engaging Others

The name Social Architecting was purposefully chosen to convey the idea that each individual can do his or her part to be a bridge-building engineer in one-on-one relationships, work groups, and organizations. It is about taking action intentionally to create good dialogue across differences and to communicate in ways that resolve conflict effectively. It also means structuring a work environment that gets the best of everyone's talents and skills and fosters creativity in an emotionally safe space. Whether you are an employee, a team member, a manager, or a leader, being a Social Architect is a critical competency in making the work environment a healthy, rich, and productive place for all.

The four skills in Social Architecting are the following:

- Serving as a cultural interpreter
- Communicating effectively
- Resolving conflicts in diverse settings
- Structuring a synergistic and compelling environment

Serving as a cultural interpreter

If you can visualize yourself as a bridge in this architectural metaphor, then you will understand this concept. Managers have to bring people together. If they can't do that or don't do that, work may not get done, and good ideas might not flow. As a manager/cultural interpreter, you really become a behavioral/idea translator who is helping people gain understanding where they don't have it and get a new set of lenses for a broader picture when the view would otherwise be limited.

Communicating effectively and resolving conflicts in diverse settings

To go back to our ice cream analogy that was introduced early in this chapter, there are many flavors, or ways of communicating. Personal and cultural differences abound, and they influence not only how you communicate but also how you solve problems. Being able to adapt and communicate effectively with multiple styles as well as to resolve conflict is key.

Structuring a synergistic and compelling environment

One of our prime goals is to have people go from saying about their work life, "Thank God it's Friday" to "Thank God I'm here." The latter statement is a

Taking the Emotional Intelligence and Diversity Quiz

Which aspects of emotional intelligence have you developed? Which do you need to develop further?

	Yes	No	Sometimes

Affirmative Introspection—Taking a Look Inside

1. Do you know what pushes your buttons when dealing with different staff members and clients?

2. Have you spent time analyzing the impact of your values and beliefs on your behavior and expectations of others?

3. Are you comfortable with yourself no matter with whom you are working or whom you are serving?

Self-Governance—Getting a Handle on Your Feelings

4. Are you adaptable and flexible in the face of change?

5. Can you manage your discomfort when you are uncertain about what to do?

6. When you face resistance or difficulties, is your "self-talk" affirming and realistic?

Intercultural Literacy—Reading Others Accurately

7. Do you know about the cultural differences that influence the behavior of your staff and customers or clients?

8. Can you see the benefits even in norms and practices you don't like?

9. Can you put yourself in others' positions and see things from their point of view?

Activity 2 (continued)   **Yes**   **No**   **Sometimes**

Social Architecting—Enrolling and Engaging Others

10. When you see a behavior that challenges your expectations, do you consider multiple explanations?

11. Can you adapt your communication style to be effective with a wide array of colleagues and clients?

12. Are you able to create welcoming and engaging environments in your department and organization?

---

great indicator that a compelling environment exists. There are many ways to create a compelling environment, and Chapter 6 on Social Architecting will provide the map and make the how-tos clear.

As you look at each concept in more depth, please keep the mirror and map metaphors fresh in your mind. Some pictures of yourself will be reinforced and some new ones will be created. You will gain knowledge, insight, and a fresh perspective, and when you do, it will be time to get your map ready. We offer many viable paths for creating a more effective you.

Start by taking a look in the mirror using the Emotional Intelligence and Diversity Quiz in Activity 2. It will give you insight into which aspects of emotional intelligence you have developed and which you need to develop further.

The Next Steps

The Emotional Intelligence and Diversity Quiz is an initial step in helping you understand yourself better. The more "Yes" answers you have, the more you have already developed your emotional intelligence. Take some time to think about your responses. Your "Sometimes" answers let you know when you respond in a healthy and effective way but also when there are other circumstances where you could be more effective for yourself and others. The importance of the "Sometimes" answers is that they give you a chance to see patterns. Are there people or circumstances that bring out the best in you? Are there people or circumstances that bring out the worst? You can begin to differentiate and take the "Sometimes" data forward with you as you learn more about each component. The "No" answers are clear opportunities for growth. Please see them as that. "No" answers are not indictments—rather, they are opportunities.

If you do your part to take a good, thoughtful look at your quiz responses, the rest of this book will give you insights, answers, tools, and skills that will liberate you. Read on.

3

Affirmative Introspection — Taking a Look Inside

Knowing yourself is a crucial element of emotional intelligence. It is a skill developed, in part, through the practice of what we call the "Affirmative Introspection" dimension of the EID Model. You probably already know that you cannot change others, that you can only change yourself. But you cannot do this without the courage to take a look inside—to be honest and see your behavior and intentions with clarity.

This dimension is purposely placed first because it focuses on self-knowledge, a crucial starting point before you take action and deal with others. It involves three components.

Components of Affirmative Introspection

- Knowing what makes you tick

- Being comfortable in your own skin

- Being aware of your own biases and hot buttons

Each of these components, in its own way, will contribute to making you more affirmatively introspective—and more ready to deal productively with diversity at work.

The techniques and tools in this chapter will help you bring more depth to your communication and develop better relationships with others on the job. You will have a greater repertoire of choices in your interactions with others instead of allowing yourself to go with the habitual choice, and this repertoire will ultimately enhance your effectiveness. You will also be able to identify those aspects at work that trigger innate, impulsive reactions. By being aware of those intangibles that push your hot buttons, you can better manage them. You will understand yourself more profoundly, which will enable you to deal with questions such as the following:

- How can I understand myself better so that I can leverage my strengths and minimize my weaknesses in dealing with my colleagues and staff?

- What are some of my cross-cultural and diversity blind spots that keep me from hiring and promoting qualified candidates?

- Why do some situations at work suddenly trigger anger or anxiety to the point where I feel "emotionally hijacked"?

- Do my values match my behaviors in my dealings with others in the workplace?

The Value of Affirmative Introspection

Affirmative Introspection is the dimension of the Emotional Intelligence and Diversity Model that brings awareness and understanding of yourself and helps you choose more effective responses and paths. It is human nature to try to conceal some hard truths from yourself and others. Affirmative Introspection is the ability to take an honest look inward, with curiosity in a non-judgmental way. It involves the ability to gain insights into the multiple layers of your experiences and to accept what you see, both your strengths and your vulnerabilities. The philosophy behind this dimension is that you can broaden introspective awareness without self-judgment.

Affirmation describes the process of developing acceptance of self and others. It requires a suspension of judgment, with none of the customary denial, shame, or guilt that accompanies new self-awareness—particularly when this awareness involves seeing aspects that you don't like. Striving for self-acceptance opens the road for new possibilities.

Introspection refers to the skill of exploring who you are, how you became that way, and what values, norms, and principles account for the way you interpret behavior and respond to others.

Affirmative Introspection is the dimension that brings the awareness of self that is necessary as a first step in becoming an emotionally intelligent individual in a diverse world.

Emotionally intelligent leaders embrace the Affirmative Introspective perspective. They invite their employees to get "360-degree feedback" and to incorporate that feedback not as a punitive force but as a catalyst for growth and development. The reason many leaders and managers spend energy on encouraging their staff to develop self-curiosity and self-awareness is that they realize shedding light on one's own behavior, feelings, and intentions will make the resulting behaviors and choices not only right but also more effective.

The Critical Perfectionist

Daniel is a production manager at a manufacturing company. He is very analytical, both an action and a bottom-line leader. Detail-oriented, he prides himself on his zero-error tolerance policy. His need for perfection has helped him deliver on his commitments. Asked why he was referring Daniel for coaching, his supervisor reported to us that he noted poor retention among Daniel's staff and believed that this was related to his poor interpersonal skills. Although Daniel is technically competent, his subordinates have complained in exit interviews about his critical demeanor, often adding that his unit was characterized by low morale.

Daniel was raised by a highly competitive and demanding father. His father expected perfection from Daniel and similarly had zero tolerance for mistakes. Through introspection during coaching, Daniel realized that his supervisory behavior mirrored his father's and that he had developed an internal belief system that alienated and demotivated subordinates. Understanding the underlying reasons for his approach was key for Daniel in helping to choose a less critical and more supportive way of relating to subordinates. Daniel's introspection resulted in more effectiveness for everyone: better management of his own disappointments made him less irritable and more accepting of others. As a result, he developed stronger connections with team members, who in turn felt more inspired by him. The work group became stronger, resulting in a more successful organization with less employee turnover.

Many managers want their employees to be more open to feedback and less defensive when receiving it. Affirmative Introspection skills can help you develop a culture of nondefensiveness and curiosity in the workplace. One of our favorite practitioners of this aspect of emotional intelligence is Richard Phillips Feynman, winner of the Nobel Prize in Physics in 1965 and author of *The Pleasure of Finding Things Out* (Cambridge, MA: Perseus Books, 1990). Feynman created work environments in diverse settings and countries in which employees and students sought self-knowledge through self-exploration and feedback from others. This was achieved in a low-pressure and pleasurable climate.

You might be wondering if people can develop introspective capacities. Working with people at all levels in many types of organizations, we know that people can train themselves to develop introspective skills. You just need to assume a "position of curiosity"; in other words, dedicate some time to looking inward at how you are "wired," and then commit to following the Affirmative Introspection steps below.

Step 1: Identify a behavior, feeling, or situation over which you would like to have more control and mastery.

Step 2: Suspend all judgment about your feelings, your thoughts, and your discoveries.

Step 3: Ask yourself what is the relevance of the situation or behavior you are trying to understand.

Step 4: Identify the impacts, both negative and positive, that these behaviors or situations are having on you and your life.

Step 5: Identify the different feelings that these behaviors or situations are eliciting in you. For a vocabulary of emotions, refer to the table on pages 48 and 49.

Step 6: Clarify the lessons you are learning from these discoveries and commit to applying them in order to become more effective at work and in your personal life.

An essential part of the introspective process is having an extensive "emotional vocabulary," in other words, finding words to describe and communicate your feelings. Having a limited vocabulary to express emotions makes your communication vague, general, and ambiguous. Acquiring a richer vocabulary of emotions helps you feel clearer about your ideas and results in better connection to the message you are communicating. Look at the following table and circle ten emotions you have experienced at work in the past week.

The Introspective Process in Action

Two scenarios show how the introspective process works:

Situation 1: A co-worker of yours has a different interpretation regarding whose responsibility it is to do a certain task.

> **Step 1: Identify a behavior, feeling, or situation.** Take a deep breath and assume a position of curiosity regarding the intensity of anger that you feel toward your co-worker. Is it because you interpret his behavior as trying to avoid doing his job and manipulating the situation to dump more work on you?

> **Step 2: Suspend all judgment.** Make a commitment to suspend judgment toward your co-worker by using the "holding technique," in which you command judgmental thoughts and strong feelings to stay in a holding pattern and assure them that you will come back to them later. Assume a position of curiosity.

> **Step 3: Ask yourself what is the relevance.** You realize that this situation is so important because you have a strong belief or core value that others should be reliable, accountable, and trustworthy.

> **Step 4: Identify the different impacts.** One impact is practical: you need to be "right" but also effective in dealing with your co-workers. Another impact is your need to create a win-win solution.

> **Step 5: Identify the different feelings.** You feel anger toward your co-worker, a feeling of strength fueled by your commitment toward assertiveness in taking care of your needs, anxiety about not knowing how to resolve this conflict, and shame about your response to your co-workers.

Vocabulary of Emotions

Fear	Anger	Shame	Confusion	Happiness
alarmed	annoyed	contrite	doubtful	buoyant
apprehensive	belligerent	embarrassed	dubious	carefree
cautious	bitter	humiliated	hesitant	cheerful
dismayed	cross	ill at ease	indecisive	contented
distrustful	enraged	inferior	mixed-up	ecstatic
edgy	envious	mortified	perplexed	elated
fearful	frustrated	regretful	preoccupied	enthusiastic
hesitant	fuming	rejected	questioning	excited
horrified	furious	remorseful	skeptical	exhilarated
insecure	grumpy	self-doubting	suspicious	festive
nervous	indignant	shameful	torn	giddy
petrified	inflamed	useless	unbelieving	glad
pressured	irate	worthless	wavering	hilarious
scared	irritated			inspired
shaky	jealous			jolly
suspicious	offended			jubilant
terrified	resentful			lighthearted
threatened	sullen			optimistic
timid				playful
worried				pleased
				satisfied
				serene
				silly
				sparkling
				spirited
				thrilled
				vivacious

Vocabulary of Emotions

Eagerness	Hurt	Love	Sadness	Sensation
anticipating	aching	affectionate	blah	alive
avid	afflicted	ardent	choked up	breathless
earnest	crushed	close	depressed	broken
excited	despairing	compassion	disappointed	clammy
expectant	devastated	concerned	discontented	empty
intent	distressed	desirous	dismal	frisky
keen	heartbroken	devoted	dreary	hard
proud	injured	enamored	dull	hollow
zealous	isolated	excited	flat	immobilized
	offended	fascinated	gloomy	light
	pained	fondness	heavy-hearted	nauseated
	suffering	generous	in the dumps	numb
	tortured	grateful	low	paralyzed
		passionate	melancholy	repulsed
		soft	moody	sensual
		tender	mournful	sluggish
		warm	somber	split
			sorrowful	stretched
			unhappy	strong
			weepy	tense
				tired
				uptight
				weak
				weary

Source: Jorge Cherbosque, Lee Gardenswartz, and Anita Rowe, *Affirmative Introspection Workbook* (Los Angeles: Emotional Intelligence and Diversity Institute, 2005).

Step 6: Clarify the lessons. You learned that your interpretation of being manipulated is a hot button for you, that you need to question your assumptions toward others' intentions more often, and that the line between assertiveness and aggression is a fine one and can be crossed easily.

Situation 2: A co-worker has recently taken time off for a religious holiday.

Step 1: Identify a behavior, feeling, or situation. Ask yourself why you are so annoyed at his taking time off for religious reasons. Is it because of your own feelings toward religion? Is it because of his religion in particular? Or is it because of your strong work ethic?

Step 2: Suspend all judgment. When you step back and assume a position of curiosity, you discover that you are trying to impose your own values on others.

Step 3: Ask yourself what is the relevance. You realize that this situation is important to you because you have a strong value that religious beliefs should not play any role in the workplace.

Step 4: Identify the different impacts. You realize that you have strong beliefs on this issue and that it is creating great resentment and distance toward your co-worker.

Step 5: Identify the different feelings. Thinking about the situation, you discover that you have some discomfort with and distrust of people who have strong religious beliefs because you were raised in a religious home yourself. You notice feelings of anxiety because your co-worker's beliefs and practices are different from yours and are largely unfamiliar to you.

Step 6: Clarify the lessons. You learned that you are trying to impose your values on others as if they should be the "right ones," and you become aware of your discomfort stemming from unfamiliar religious customs and practices.

This introspective process should bring you a greater sense of clarity and ease, along with a greater sense of optimism and resilience generated by your ability to learn from your past and from your affirming, nonjudgmental attitude. Now try practicing the introspective process yourself in Activity 3.

Activity 3

Applying the Introspective Process

Think about an important situation at work that generated strong feelings and about which you would like more insight. Then follow the introspective process. Write your observations below:

Step 1: Identify a behavior, feeling, or situation over which you would like to have more control and mastery. Ask yourself, "I wonder why I reacted in such a way."

_____

_____

Step 2: Suspend all judgment about your feelings, thoughts, and discoveries.

_____

_____

Step 3: Ask yourself, "What is the relevance of the situation or behavior I am trying to understand. Why does it matter so much?"

_____

_____

Step 4: Identify the different impacts, both negative and positive, that these behaviors or situations are having on you and your life.

_____

_____

Step 5: Identify the different feelings that these behaviors or situations are eliciting in you. For a vocabulary of emotions, refer to the table on pages 48 and 49.

_____

_____

Step 6: Clarify the lessons you are learning from these discoveries, and commit to applying them in order to become more effective at work and in your personal life.

_____

_____

Now that you know the introspective process, you can use it as you develop the three elements of Affirmative Introspection:

- Knowing what makes you tick

- Being comfortable in your own skin

- Being aware of your own biases and hot buttons

Knowing What Makes You Tick

The past isn't dead. It isn't even the past.
—WILLIAM FAULKNER

Reflect for a moment. Think about what you do when you want to energize yourself. What makes you feel excited? What is worth waking up for? What are key motivators for your co-workers? What are their core values? Knowing what makes you and others tick is one of the most useful skills a manager can develop because it is a crucial component of motivating employees from diverse backgrounds. It also helps you build trust and develop connections. Knowing who you really are, what motivates you, what brings you down, what your expectations of yourself and others are, and what shapes and influences those needs and expectations is vital if you want to be not only right but also effective.

Being aware of the messages you received from your childhood, your formative experiences, your values, and your cultural customs is critical. Human beings are wired to repeat their histories and create self-fulfilling prophecies. If you don't examine and test those beliefs and thoughts consciously, you will have problems with managing diversity in the workplace. In her popular book *The Secret*, Rhonda Byrne teaches us that all individuals have core beliefs that are powerful in attracting outcomes—either positive or negative—in their lives. She calls this phenomenon "the law of attraction." If you have a core belief that there is abundance in the world, you will attract many opportunities for growth and development. If you have a core belief of scarcity, you will not only perceive limitations at work, you will attract barriers and obstacles along any growth path.

Core Beliefs

Your core beliefs are at the heart of what makes you tick. The core beliefs that guide your life and decision making are attitudes that tend to be shaped by your cultural and family experiences. Some of these are positive and facilitate interaction with others. Others are maladaptive. They block growth and contaminate reality, resulting in suspicion, fear, isolation, avoidance, and impaired productivity. Below is a list of some core beliefs or attitudes that you and your co-workers may have. These core beliefs can have a major effect on behavior and interactions in the workplace. Positive beliefs can help create a strong, healthy environment, while negative beliefs may lead to isolation and lack of productivity. Identify the beliefs that resonate with you by checking them off in Checklist 2. Then think about how these core beliefs affect how you feel about yourself and others and how you interact with others. Also think about which core beliefs you see in your employees and how their core beliefs may play out in the workplace.

Being aware of your core beliefs, both the positive and maladaptive ones, may lead you to assume a more strategic attitude toward your life, opening new possibilities and generating feelings of passion, energy, love, and gratitude instead of feelings of isolation, depression, oppression, and doom at work.

Another way to become aware of what makes you tick is to identify your core values. Your values can change with time and may reflect different developmental needs. At one point in your work life, you may value maximum independence and opportunity for upward mobility. At another point, job security may be a top choice. Knowing the core values of your employees can be extremely valuable to you as a manager. This is especially true if you are managing individuals from diverse ethnic and cultural backgrounds. With good intention you may be guided by the Golden Rule: "Treat others as *you* want to be treated." However, you might find it more helpful to use the Platinum Rule: "Treat others as *they* want to be treated."

The importance of knowing the core values of your co-workers is illustrated by this story.

Laverne managed a manufacturing plant. She wanted to reward her employee Diane by promoting her to supervisor and offering her a beautiful corporate

Checklist 2

Core Beliefs in the Workplace

POSITIVE CORE BELIEFS IN THE WORKPLACE

- ☐ I trust and can rely on my co-workers and supervisors.

- ☐ I value the diversity of my co-workers and believe that if we leverage our differences, we will create synergistic solutions.

- ☐ I can be open to feedback and use it as a tool for self-growth and development.

- ☐ Life is full of abundance. I see many opportunities for fulfilling my core needs at work.

- ☐ Life is an adventure. I can take risks when opportunities present themselves.

- ☐ Work can be joyful and invigorating.

- ☐ I can learn from my mistakes and avoid similar errors without feeling defensive or ashamed of them.

- ☐ I can have respectful and pro-ductive dialogues with employees holding different points of view.

- ☐ I enjoy exposing myself to different cultures and languages. I believe the exposure will provide me with a wealth of perspectives that will ultimately benefit my work.

NEGATIVE CORE BELIEFS IN THE WORKPLACE

- ☐ I can never be part of a work group.

- ☐ You cannot trust anyone, even your family.

- ☐ The more energy we expend on diversity issues, the more it separates us.

- ☐ I will never get what I want.

- ☐ Understanding others from different cultures means we will excuse poor behavior.

- ☐ Work is something I do to pay my bills. I can hardly wait for my retirement.

- ☐ My supervisors and others with authority do not really care about me. They use me only so that they can look good.

- ☐ I am threatened by changes at work. It was so much better in the good old days.

- ☐ This new initiative will lead nowhere. It is just another "flavor of the month."

- ☐ It is too late to fulfill my dreams. I missed the boat!

office. Diane did not enjoy this reward because she had thrived on the connection she had with her peers. As supervisor, she felt physically and emotionally isolated from her former support group.

When you understand the importance of knowing the key values and experiences of your staff members, you can better help them navigate through the inevitable difficulties they will experience on the job. For example, managers who are really in touch with their employees will be able to recognize the values threatened by an imposed organizational change. One person may be unnerved by the loss of relationships, while another may worry about the loss of job security or creative input.

We are often called upon as consultants to help managers create a respectful workplace. We usually start by inviting employees to identify and share formative experiences that have contributed to their philosophy of life, their values, and their customs and habits, as well as the experiences that led them to their occupations. Typically, after only fifteen minutes of sharing what makes them tick, they feel not only connected but transformed. Participants tell us that they originally saw only the introductory "pages" to one another's lives. After sharing their experiences, they saw many other pages, many other dimensions to one another, leading to respect, admiration, and empathy. Some leaders see these kind of experiences as "soft," a waste of time that does not contribute to the bottom line. They are, however, far from being correct. In order to produce, people need to feel connected to others, to know and trust one another so they can be open to others' feedback and input. Once employees achieve this kind of connection, real, synergistic, and creative ideas can emerge.

In order to better understand who you are, we encourage you to identify your own core values and the values of others. A good way to get to know your colleagues and employees and what makes them tick is by asking them to identify and prioritize their core values. The list of values in Activity 4 may be useful for you in starting a dialogue about the role values play in each employee's work life. Be sure to do these activities first yourself so you can be a full participant in the discussion.

Activity 4

Knowing Your Values

From the following list of values, circle five that are currently among your top priorities. Then select a co-worker, ask him or her to do the exercise, and also choose what you perceive to be his or her five main values. Selecting a co-worker from a diverse background might be especially instructive here.

Fairness Defending equitable treatment of yourself and others	**Honesty** Speaking or presenting material in a straightforward and truthful manner	**Tolerance** Respecting others; accepting differences	**Courage** Standing up for your beliefs when it is difficult to do so; overcoming fear
Integrity Acting in congruence with your beliefs	**Forgiveness** Being able to pardon others and let go of hurt	**Peace** Practicing nonviolent conflict resolution	**Environment** Practicing respect for the Earth's future
Challenge Testing physical limits; taking risks	**Self-acceptance** Having self-respect; maintaining self-esteem in the face of negative feedback	**Tradition** Respecting the ways things have always been done	**Security** Being free from worry; feeling safe; being risk-free
Knowledge Seeking intellectual stimulation, new ideas, truth, and understanding	**Adventure** Accepting challenges; taking risks; testing limits	**Creativity** Finding new ways to do things; innovating	**Personal Growth** Committing to continual interpersonal and intrapersonal learning; developing new social skills; having self-awareness
Recognition Getting noticed for effective efforts	**Authority** Having the power to direct events; make things happen	**Power** Having control over events, people, and things; implementing plans	**Competition** Winning; doing better or achieving more than others

Inner Harmony Being free from inner conflict; being integrated; having serenity	**Spiritual Growth** Having a relationship to a higher purpose; believing in a divine being	**Belonging** Being connected to and liked by others; identifying with a group	**Diplomacy** Finding common ground with difficult people and situations; resolving conflict
Teamwork Cooperating with others toward a common goal	**Helping** Taking care of others; doing what they need	**Communication** Maintaining open dialogue; exchanging views	**Friendship** Having close companionship; having ongoing relationships
Consensus Making decisions you feel the group needs or wants	**Respect** Showing consideration; regarding others with honor	**Stability** Having certainty; having predictability; following a time-honored path	**Neatness** Being tidy; being orderly; being clean
Rationality Being consistent; being logical; being clear; reasoning; being unemotional	**Health** Maintaining and enhancing physical and mental well-being	**Pleasure** Having personal satisfaction; having enjoyment, delight	**Play** Being fun; being light; having spontaneity
Prosperity Flourishing; being well-off; being able to afford desires	**Family** Taking care of and spending time with loved ones	**Appearance** Looking good; dressing well; keeping fit	**Intimacy/Love** Having a deep emotional, spiritual connection
Aesthetic Desiring beauty; pleasing the senses	**Community** Connecting to a group of people who share physical space or are joined by a common purpose	**Competence** Being good at what you do; being capable; being effective	**Achievement** Successfully completing visible tasks or projects
Self-control Being self-disciplined; being restrained	**Perseverance** Pushing through to the end; completing tasks even with obstacles in the way	**Advancement** Getting ahead; being ambitious; aspiring to higher levels	**Intellectual Status** Pursuing a discipline or other extensive knowledge, logic, reasoning

Behaving with emotional intelligence means that your values and your behaviors match. Complete Activity 5 to assess how closely your behaviors reflect your values and to more closely align your values and actions.

Activity 5

Living Your Values

List the top five values you identified in Activity 4, and check how closely your behavior reflects each one.

My Five Most Important Values Are:	My behavior consistently reflects this value	My behavior partially reflects this value	My behavior does not reflect this value
1.			
2.			
3.			
4.			
5.			

Now list some steps you can take to bring your values and actions closer together.

_____

_____

_____

_____

_____

_____

_____

_____

_____

_____

_____

Activity 6

Comparing Values at Work

What are your values? How do they compare with others' values?

My Values	Values of my co-worker or supervisor

To further refine your introspective tools, refer to the core values you listed in Activity 5, and think about the formative experiences that may have contributed to the development of these values. In Activity 6, compare your values with those of a co-worker or supervisor and spend some time discussing the similarities and differences of your formative experiences.

How can you use this knowledge of your and others' work values? Knowing what makes you tick can help you better understand the kind of work environment that is best suited to you and the kinds of behaviors that will motivate you and your employees to perform optimally. Knowing your employees' life stories and letting them know yours not only builds deeper connections but also helps you design an environment that brings out the best in them.

Maps to Help You Know What Makes You Tick

By knowing what makes you tick, you can communicate more clearly who you are and why you respond the way you do. The result? Your life and work will be more satisfying. You will also sharpen your ability to choose different, more effective behaviors in response to life's infinite challenges. Take the plunge into greater awareness. Aim for more clarity about what makes you tick. The following tips represent maps that can guide you toward understanding what makes you tick.

Map 1: Know and choose joy. What makes life worth living for you? What is an instant joy in your life? Make a list of people and activities or experiences that give you the most joy. Set a date for the next time you will pursue a few of those activities and choose one a week to do for the next month.

Map 2: Know your slogan. Who are you? What do you stand for? What makes you tick? Create a bumper sticker that encapsulates your values, your style, who you are, and what matters most to you.

Map 3: Know your shapers. External experiences and the media play a role in forming who you are and what makes you tick. Identify a person, an experience, a book, and a film that were influential in shaping you. Write about the values and lessons you learned from each and how they influence you today. Notice any similarities there may be among the values.

Map 4: Prevent energy shortages. Energy comes from internal motivation driven by your desires and values. List three things that fill your energy pump and three that drain it. Make a commitment to filling that pump with at least one activity choice each week and eliminating one drainer. Identify your start date.

Map 5: Talk the talk. Enriching your life comes, in large part, from being able to delve deeply into your emotions. Help yourself in this process by finding a time each day to identify an additional word that describes a feeling and use it in talking about an experience you had that day. Exhilarated, dismayed, motivated, or inspired might be your word. Don't forget: variety is the spice of life. Pepper your sentences with new feeling words every day.

Map 6: Find your "unicability." "Unicability" is our term for the place where your talents and passions merge. Identify two places or times in your life when these two came together at work. Then pinpoint the key feelings you had at those times. Think of a way to create another opportunity where you can experience this merging of talent and passion.

Being Comfortable in Your Own Skin

We can travel the world over but we take ourselves with us.
—RALPH WALDO EMERSON

How often do you wish you were a different height, a different weight, a different—well, you name it! Achieving comfort in your own skin can be difficult. In order to become effective in accepting, valuing, and dealing with others, you need to be aware of and open to those aspects within yourself that you have difficulty accepting. There is no escape! Bottom line: the path to loving, respecting, and accepting others is to love, respect, and accept yourself first. Emotional intelligence skills are oriented toward bringing you to awareness of particular aspects of yourself that are not in harmony with your self-image.

Internal Messages

You internalize messages that come from family, friends, school, and the media. These messages either help you feel good about yourself, which encourages you to integrate them into your personality, or uncomfortable, which leads you to disown those parts. An important element of Emotional Intelligence and Diversity is not only becoming aware of the different aspects of ourselves with which we don't feel comfortable but learning ways to merge aspects of our ideal and real selves.

Emotional intelligence skills in this area can help you become aware of those aspects with which you are not comfortable. This is important because when you are in harmony with yourself, you create an environment that is comfortable for others. We have heard many employees admire leaders who project a genuine acceptance of themselves, their strengths, and vulnerabilities, and who are willing to look at their imperfections with curiosity.

Carl Rogers, a pioneer of humanistic psychology, made this particular quality the center of his therapeutic approach. He believed that unconditional acceptance (which he called "unconditional positive regard") is one of the greatest gifts you can give to both yourself and to others. He said that this unconditional acceptance is the environment in which you allow others to feel safe and accepted and give them permission to take risks and be as creative as possible. In his book *On Becoming a Person* (Boston: Houghton Mifflin, 1961), Carl Rogers states: "In my early professional life, I was asking the question: How can I treat, or change this person? Now, I would phrase the question in this way: How can I provide a relationship which this person may use for his own personal growth?" We believe that the more acceptance people feel toward themselves and others, the more likely they are to create productive work environments. By acceptance, we don't mean a passive, unexamined, and compliant life. We mean quite the opposite: a life spent actively looking at ourselves with warm regard for our personal assets and imperfections, a life spent seeking insight into the ways in which our assets and imperfections affect our lives and the lives of others.

The fundamental question that this dimension of emotional intelligence asks is, "Do I accept myself and others, or do I accept conditionally—silently or openly disapproving of others whom I perceive as threatening?"

Paradoxically, the more you free yourself from your inner critical voice and from the external evaluations of others, the more you permit yourself to recognize that the center of responsibility for behavior lies within you. This point is crucial in a supervisory relationship. If you don't need to spend energy fighting for self-approval or the approval of others, you are left to contemplate your own truth and, by owning it, take full responsibility for your choices and allow others to take responsibility for theirs.

When you are uncomfortable with aspects of your personality, you frequently project them onto others in a critical way. For instance, if you are not comfortable with your own need to control others or your environment, you might project this need onto others and accuse them of trying to control you. If you feel critical of your intellectual abilities, you might project your discomfort onto someone else and put him down for making a "dumb comment." Psychologists call this tendency of transferring aspects of yourself that you don't like onto others as "projection" or "negative transference." Emotionally intelligent leaders help employees embrace their personal power and discover hidden or disowned gifts and talents kept at bay because of years of criticism and self-doubt.

You can probably understand the dangers of projecting onto others those aspects of your personality with which you are uncomfortable. Completing Activity 7 will help you explore your level of comfort in several dimensions of diversity.

Assessing Your Comfort in Your Own Skin

How comfortable are you in your own skin? Use the following questions to assess your comfort level.

1. How comfortable am I with my physical appearance? Are there any aspects that are difficult for me to accept?

What are they?

_____

_____

2. How comfortable am I with my intellectual abilities? Are there any aspects that are difficult for me to accept?

What are they?

_____

_____

3. How comfortable am I with my chosen profession or occupation? Are there any aspects that are difficult for me to accept?

What are they?

_____

_____

4. How comfortable am I with authority figures? Are there things about them that are difficult for me to trust?

What are they?

_____

_____

Enhancing self-acceptance and ease is a continuous process. We have created the following maps in order to guide you in the right direction.

Maps to Help You Develop Comfort in Your Own Skin

To be more effective with others, you first need to accept, value, and appreciate yourself. This means accepting not only your strengths but also aspects you don't necessarily like and might wish were different. Making peace with those aspects is the real test of becoming comfortable with who you are. To increase your comfort, try the following tips:

Map 1: Take a risk. Being comfortable in your own skin means that you can put yourself in unfamiliar territory. Take a trip with an outdoor expert, a trip that pushes you beyond your comfort zone. Ride the whitewater rapids, hike the Andes, or skydive. Engage in any activity that raises your anxiety a little. Doing so will stretch your limits and increase your comfort with your physical self.

Map 2: Learn to say no. To risk rejection by saying no to someone is a way of taking care of yourself. You will see how it can help you to feel okay about yourself. Find areas in your life where you need to give yourself permission to say no. Then do it! You'll find that your feelings of resentment will diminish as you start saying no to things you really do not want to do.

Map 3: Be strategic in seeking feedback. Getting a more complete picture of yourself can help you know and accept the full you. Identify a person you respect and trust. Ask that person to identify one area for your further development and then give you feedback on how you can strengthen that area to be more effective in your interactions.

Map 4: Check out your reflection. Most people, even the most beautiful or handsome, can easily point out their physical flaws. Work on becoming more accepting of your own physical self. Take a look in the mirror, preferably a full-length mirror, and identify five things about your appearance that you like. Acknowledge them aloud. Repeat them at least one more time.

Map 5: See with compassionate eyes. Self-acceptance requires that you be kind to yourself. Think of an aspect of yourself with which you're not comfortable. Imagine that this characteristic belongs to someone whom you love. List three positive messages you could tell that person about this quality; then tell yourself.

Map 6: Know what is magical about you. Recognizing your own impact on others is a key element of self-acceptance. Ask a family member, co-worker, and boss each to tell you, very specifically, three to five ways that you create or bring magic to an environment where they see you interact.

Being Aware of Your Own Biases and Hot Buttons

The life that is unexamined is not worth living.
—SOCRATES

Stereotypes, biases, and hot buttons are the opinions, beliefs, and knee-jerk reactions that all people have about others. Usually they are so charged that people don't want to acknowledge them. The film *Guess Who's Coming to Dinner* became popular in the United States in the 1960s because it touched on this truth. Which of the following might be a hot button for you?

- You receive twenty e-mails a day from the same person.

- You are greeted negatively at an interview because your looks don't match expectations.

- Others assume you play golf because that is where major decisions are made.

- A colleague shows up twenty-five minutes late for a meeting with you.

Hot buttons, yours and others', are pressed at work. You may also set off hot buttons in others. For example, you may be a person who thrives on speaking loudly and having many visitors, yet your officemate prefers working in peace and quiet without disruption. Or your detail-oriented ways may push buttons for some who see such behavior as perverse micromanagement.

Feeling "emotionally hijacked" (a term coined by Daniel Goleman) is another way of saying you are experiencing a knee-jerk reaction, a strong emotional response when you feel that someone is pushing your buttons. There are some biological factors responsible for this reaction.

Scientists have known for some time that the prefrontal lobes of the brain are involved in the processing of emotion. It has not been until recently that scientists have understood the precise role of the prefrontal cortex. It turns out that it is not the site at which emotion is formed but the area where it is reasoned and processed. The prefrontal cortex, part of the neocortex (what emotional intelligence theorist Daniel Goleman refers to as the "thinking brain"), interacts with the more primitive part of the brain, the limbic system (referred to by Goleman as "the emotional brain") and its amygdala. These are all key players in people's emotional lives.

Recently Joseph LeDoux, a neuroscientist at the Center for Neural Science at New York University, made a landmark discovery about the relationship and interaction of the emotional and thinking brains. He found that the emotional brain gets the information first. In the event of a crisis, the emotional brain may react before the thinking brain receives the information and can consider options. Goleman refers to this common phenomenon as "emotional hijacking."[1]

The following story looks closely at how the emotional hijacking process can play a role in the workplace.

The Retaliatory E-mail

Yvette, a director of a human resources program, described an incident of emotional hijacking from her own experience. A colleague's e-mail criticizing her roundly for a lack of attention to detail and follow-through made her instantly angry and ashamed. She interpreted it as humiliating, because the message had been copied to other managers in the workplace. Yvette sent a nasty and aggressive e-mail in response, copying the e-mail to the same group of colleagues. When Yvette felt calmer, she reread the original e-mail and realized that she had misunderstood its intent. She regretted her impulsive reaction and her humiliation of her colleague in turn. Yvette's coach helped her develop a technique for responding to triggers (in this case, perceived humiliation) that could produce emotionally hijacked states such as the impulsive behavior she exhibited. Her coach suggested that should such situations arise in the future (perceived humiliation), she should write an e-mail without sending it, get some distance from the situation, reread it, and then, if she chooses, send it.

It is important to understand the reactions generated by your own hot buttons. By doing so, you will see that many of them stem from a need for control in your environment and in your life, as well as the need to be included and appreciated by others. It is helpful to ask yourself what needs for control or approval a given situation touches. In this way you can begin to behave more rationally.

In diverse environments, biases against those who display different behaviors and norms may push our buttons. Look at the behaviors listed below and check off any that are difficult for you. Then begin analyzing why they are difficult for you.

- People who interrupt you before you finish speaking

- People who are late to meetings

- People who talk too much about their own accomplishments

- People who smile all the time

- People who stand too close to you in an elevator

- Co-workers who insist on paying only their share when you go to lunch as a team

- Customers who expect you to fulfill a last-minute request

- Situations where bilingual information is provided

- People who hire and promote relatives and friends at work

It is only from your awareness of these biases and hot buttons that you can choose to react to them in a nonexplosive and more effective way. Once you recognize hot buttons, the next step is to de-escalate your reactions to them.

De-escalating Your Reactions to Hot Buttons

You can de-escalate your reactions to hot buttons by looking inward and analyzing what you see. The following steps should be useful in governing your emotions in the face of circumstances that are difficult for you.

Step 1: Analyze the threat to your being in control and receiving approval. Ask yourself: is this behavior really going to prevent me from being in control and getting approval?

Step 2: Analyze your perception of the other's intent. Ask yourself: is this person really trying to do me harm?

Step 3: Analyze the cultural implications. Ask yourself: what might be the cultural explanations for this behavior?

Step 4: Analyze your relationship with the "offender." Ask yourself: how might my response differ from person to person?

Step 5: Analyze the impact of the situation on your life. Ask yourself: what is the real, not exaggerated, impact that this has on my life?

Step 6: Analyze your power to influence the situation. Ask yourself: what can I do to improve the situation?

Let's apply these steps to the following, potentially volatile situation: Two employees from different cultural backgrounds have been sharing a small office for approximately six months. Jenny is stifling some anger at Siobhan's constant stream of visitors and frequent lengthy phone calls with extended family members. After numerous failed attempts to limit Siobhan's interruptions to her work, Jenny locks Siobhan out of the office one morning.

Step 1: Analyze the threat. Jenny must ask herself: is Siobhan's behavior really going to prevent me from being in control and getting approval? Jenny may discover that she wants Siobhan to behave in a way similar to her. She can learn to be more flexible and curious by looking for positive aspects of Siobhan's behavior.

Step 2: Analyze your perception. Jenny must ask herself: is Siobhan really trying to do me harm? Jenny may discover that Siobhan is an extroverted person who gets her energy from social interactions. Jenny is trying to impose her own personality style on Siobhan.

Step 3: Analyze the cultural implications. Jenny must ask herself: what might be the cultural explanations for Siobhan's behavior? Jenny may discover that Siobhan was raised in a collectivistic society in which keeping in touch daily with extended family and friends is not only normal but desired.

Step 4: Analyze your relationship. Jenny must ask herself: how might my response differ if this was someone I knew better or someone who was from my own culture? Jenny may discover that she feels comfortable with people who share similar cultural norms. She can learn the benefits of interacting with people from various cultures.

Step 5: Analyze the impact. Jenny must ask herself: what is the real, not exaggerated, impact that this has on my life? Jenny may discover that there are many ways to accomplish tasks at work, and others thrive by mixing the task at hand with socialization.

Step 6: Analyze your power. Jenny must ask herself: what can I do to improve the situation? Jenny could engage Siobhan in a conversation in which they can aim for a win-win resolution, such as scheduling calls and visits and allowing for quiet time.

As with Jenny's example, applying these steps can help you gain more mastery over knee-jerk reactions in hot-button situations, de-escalating potentially explosive reactions and limiting divisive behavior at work.

Maps to Help You Become Aware of Your Own Hot Buttons and Biases

All human beings have blind spots and biases, and are vulnerable to knee-jerk reactions. When you acknowledge them, you free yourself from their limits. You also create more choices and opportunities and increase comfort and connection in your world. Start shedding the limits of hot buttons and biases now by using some of these maps.

Map 1: Confront your biases. Admitting your biases and understanding what is at the bottom of each is helpful. The next time you visit a public place like a mall, sports stadium, or airport and you notice a group whose behavior bothers you, ask yourself what you actually know about this group, and what it is about their behavior that is bothersome. If you are afraid, put a specific label to that fear.

Map 2: Change your thinking. Usually when people's buttons get pushed, they simply react instead of thinking. Identify one of your most easily pushed hot buttons. How do you behave when it gets pushed? State what you think the intent is of the person doing the pushing. Then write down two other possible reasons for this person's behavior, and see if these new steps can lessen the severity of the impact.

Map 3: Neutralize your button pushers. Identify three behaviors that your employers, co-workers, and family members do that drive you crazy. Identify the possible positive intentions underlying their behavior and also think of some positive outcomes that you might experience as a result.

Map 4: You act as a hot button, too. Think of the different ways that you irritate your co-workers and supervisors. Write down one thing you can do to change a behavior of yours that is a hot button for others. If you can't identify the behavior, ask someone you trust.

Map 5: Don't judge by appearances. Reflect on a time when your bias toward someone's appearance influenced your hiring or promotion decision. Identify positive or negative consequences from your bias and write down what you learned from this experience. Consider the next time you might be able to apply the learning.

Map 6: Confront your biases. The next time you make a decision about another individual such as who to hire, promote, include, or invite, make a list of the reasons for your decision. Be honest in putting down all the reasons. Then consider how many of them are based on your biases and assumptions rather than on the facts.

The Next Steps

To be an emotionally intelligent leader, you must shed light on your own values, life experiences, and inner narratives such that you can understand yourself, expand the comfort with who you are, and accept those with whom you interact. As part of this process, you must also be equipped to identify those triggers that might set off a highly charged response in yourself and others. Complementing this awareness is the application of skills that will help govern emotions, the subject of the next chapter.

4

Self-Governance — Getting a Handle on Your Feelings

Contrary to the old adage "What you don't know can't hurt you," what you don't know can hurt you when it comes to your emotional reactions and those of your subordinates or colleagues. Chapter 3 introduced ways to learn introspection and understand yourself better, including exploring your core values and how you react to differences. Acquiring this understanding is the first step in helping you deal effectively with feelings that invariably emerge when dealing with differences. Once you realize what bothers you and why, you then need to be able to direct the energy of your emotional reactions to ambiguity and change in constructive ways—the emotional intelligence and diversity component of Self-Governance.

Building resilience and keeping a positive attitude in times of uncertainty is one of the hallmarks of emotionally intelligent leaders. These leaders have the ability to govern emotions instead of being controlled by them. It sounds easy enough, but how many times have you regretted reacting in ways that were counterproductive and that created more trouble when you were looking for a solution?

For example, identify the emotions triggered for you when

- You can't make yourself understood because no one speaks your language.

- People discount you because of your ethnicity, educational level, age, race, or gender.

- You need to be part of a team at work in which many of your peers have heavy accents.

- Someone makes incorrect assumptions about you based on stereotypes, your appearance, your physical ability, or other attributes.

- You have been unjustly accused of harassment or of showing bias.

Imagine how you felt or might feel in such situations. Irritated? Frustrated? Confused? Angry? If you have experienced any of the above situations, you may realize upon reflection that these events probably touched some of your core values. You may have had to deal with a situation that was out of your comfort zone and experience, forcing you to manage an incident and its impact on others when you felt ill prepared to do so. Humanistic psychologist Abraham Maslow has identified basic needs for human beings. He has described these in his "hierarchy of needs" as the desire to control one's environment, feel safe, and connect, belong, and feel approval from others. According to Maslow, a basic human need is to keep oneself safe and secure, both physically and emotionally. In order to do that, people need to have a sense that they can control situations. You feel safe when you control your world, making sure that situations and people function as you need them to. For example, you need the traffic light to be green often enough so that you can get to a meeting on time; you need to depend on the work of others in order to deliver your presentation in a timely and accurate manner.

Maslow also indicates that human beings need to build self-esteem, which typically develops through efforts to gain approval, respect, and positive regard from the people who matter in their lives. At times you even seek such feedback from strangers. You need your customers to love your product and service and to reciprocate with loyalty; you need your boss to respect your competence and give you a glowing performance review.[1]

Dealing with differences often shakes one or both of these pillars of safety. It is often the feeling of being out of control and unable to gain the approval of others that leads people to react emotionally. You may have feelings of frustration that you can't get your team members to understand what you want or to rally for your initiative. You may feel hurt at being discounted, disgust at being stereotyped, or rage at being treated unfairly. Each of these reactions is triggered by a sense of loss of control or approval or both. Coming to terms with these fundamental needs for control and approval are at the bottom of Self-Governance.

The three competencies of Self-Governance will help you manage your emotions so you can have more productive and effective interactions at work and in your personal life.

Components of Self-Governance

- Making ambiguity an ally

- Becoming a change master

- Getting in charge of your self-talk

The Biblical story of the brothers Cain and Abel teaches the potentially destructive power of succumbing to feelings of competition, jealousy, insecurity, and intolerance. The daily news similarly demonstrates the destructive power of such feelings. Managing their own emotions can prevent people from destroying one another and may result in a redirection of energy into building a world—or at least a workplace—where respect, synergy, and compassion rule.

Making Ambiguity an Ally

The pure and simple truth is rarely pure and never simple.

—OSCAR WILDE

If uncertainty throws you, you are not alone. Like most people, you probably want to feel in control and have your world function in predictable ways. Yet life continues to present you with situations where you are pulled in many directions and you don't know what to do. Dealing with differences often puts you in new territory, where rules and expectations are unclear and confusion about situations and their consequences abounds. This is especially true in environments of diversity, when different values and beliefs often present choices between alternatives that may have great impact on people's lives.

The following situations might occur in the workplace. How would you react?

- A co-worker makes a stereotypical comment or ethnic joke. Do you confront the person, or should you let it pass since it is the first time you have known him to make such a remark? Are you hoping your silence will keep harmony in your unit?

- You find someone's performance unsatisfactory, yet you don't want to be accused of prejudice if you give her negative feedback.

- You feel discomfort in helping a customer with a physical disability, yet you are reluctant to ask questions to learn more for fear of offending the person.

- You are uncertain whether you should bring your elderly parent to live with your family or should find him an assisted-living situation.

- You feel great conflict over whether to retire early to pursue your passion for music or to stay at your job five more years in order to achieve greater stability and higher retirement benefits in the future.

- Should you risk taking a thrilling but uncertain overseas assignment or stay on the corporate track that you know?

- Should you hire a candidate with sterling credentials but no experience or promote the employee who has experience but lacks the most up-to-date education and academic credentials?

Living with uncertainty and lack of closure in ambiguous situations is unsettling and often triggers feelings of anxiety, fear, and discomfort. One aspect of Self-Governance is the ability to manage this discomfort and, rather than look for a quick fix for the situation, sit with it long enough to work it through. An emotionally intelligent response to these uncertain situations begins by identifying the conflicting needs and values inherent in the situation and making peace with the fact that you do not always find answers immediately.

Managing Uncertainty by Using Mental Board Members

To help you confront uncertain situations, we have developed a technique that may bring more clarity and help you take the best action for yourself. Imagine that within your mind are "mental board members"—a board of directors representing different viewpoints and perspectives. The mental board members are competing for airtime as they give you advice, and some are louder than others. The purpose of this technique is to make sure you hear all the voices and can explore the advantages and consequences of each.

1. Recognize that ambiguous situations are rarely conflicts between right and wrong.

You want to understand the shades of rightness and wrongness in each choice. You may want to confront a co-worker about a stereotypic comment or the racist jokes he makes, yet you want to maintain a harmonious work relationship. Or you may want to talk to your co-workers about feeling excluded, but you don't want to come across as a whiner or a complainer.

2. Identify and pay attention to your mental board members.

Your mental board members are all the inner voices that pull you in different directions. They are the different values, principles, and "shoulds" that influence your decisions. These inner voices are powerful and are motivated by different needs. For example, some are motivated by the need for safety and stability, others by ego, and others by idealism and altruism.

You may want to confront a co-worker about his jokes, but one of your inner board members is motivated by fear and a need for stability and harmony. He may be saying, "You should avoid conflict at any cost," yet at the same time another inner board member is motivated by your commitment to valuing diversity. He may be saying, "Be congruent with your values: walk the talk."

Once you identify the different voices and their underlying motivations, go to the next step.

3. Consider the potential consequence of each choice—both positive and negative.

A positive outcome of ignoring the situation might be maintaining the status quo and preventing an argument. A negative outcome of ignoring it might be loss of self-respect, an escalation of the problem, or a missed opportunity to resolve the issue.

4. Make a choice that brings you the most positive outcome.

For example, if you confront your co-worker and approach him with curiosity rather than judgment, you satisfy your commitment for valuing diversity and acting with integrity as well as your need for keeping harmony and maintaining the relationship.

In Activity 8, practice this skill by using the mental board member technique with an ambiguous situation you are currently dealing with.

Using Mental Board Members

What are your mental board members telling you? Use this activity to evaluate your inner voices.

1. Recognize ambiguous situations you are confronting at work or in your personal life.

_____

_____

_____

2. Identify and pay attention to your mental board members' voices and their motivations.

_____

_____

_____

3. Consider the potential consequence of each choice—both positive and negative.

_____

_____

_____

4. Make a choice that brings you the most positive outcome.

_____

_____

Maps to Help You Make Ambiguity an Ally

In today's world where change is rapid and most choices are complex and layered, learning to live with uncertainty and making ambiguity an ally is critical for success. The following tips can be seen as road maps. They will be useful to you as you manage your emotions during uncertain periods when you must live with a lack of clarity.

Map 1: Make both *either* and *or* your buddies. Human beings tend to value certainty and polarized choices. Instead of rushing to premature closure and certainty when there is none, learn to consider options carefully. Get skilled at counting the possible bounty that can come from both *either* and *or* as particular directions morph into shape.

Map 2: Brainstorm. In most of life's dilemmas, there is no right or wrong answer, only different paths. To make ambiguity an ally, get a whiteboard, a chalkboard, or an easel and flipchart and open your mind. Let your ideas multiply without judging them. No matter how ridiculous the suggestions may seem, don't censor yourself. Think, create, be open, and reflect on the vast possibilities available and how all may offer something.

Map 3: Look into a crystal ball. Think carefully about an ambiguous situation you are going through and make some predictions about what some of the possible outcomes might be. Consider all the possibilities, both positive and negative. Then consider how you might deal with each. Pay particular attention to your emotional responses as you reflect on them. What do you notice? Without being limited by your past, use your history as a teacher to make good choices for your future.

Map 4: Let analysis help you through paralysis. The next time you feel stuck in an unclear situation that is pulling you in many different directions, use your analytical skills to help you. Call up the brainstormed list you just completed. Out of that absurdity may emerge something useful, unusual, and creative. As you assess each option, make a list of pros and cons. Notice the energy you feel with each. That energy will help you become unstuck, allowing you to move forward. Where there is zero energy, notice that, too.

Map 5: Count to ten. A predictable response to ambiguity is to bring closure to open-ended, unresolved issues. However, premature closure often causes us to jump to either/or views and polarized thinking. The next time you feel yourself moving too quickly toward closure because of the discomfort of uncertainty, stop and count to ten. Give yourself time to sit with the process of not knowing. Finding peace with uncertainty will help you make clear, less-pressured decisions and will almost always result in better ones.

Becoming a Change Master

Progress is impossible without change and those who
cannot change their minds cannot change anything.
—GEORGE BERNARD SHAW

A major study by the Center for Creative Leadership indicates that one of the characteristics that derails successful leaders is an inability to cope with change.[2] In our experience this is true. We have coached many workers who are afraid of the unavoidable changes they are facing, and we see how much time, effort, and energy are spent resisting and denying the changes. We are sometimes amazed by the intensity of emotions, among them fear, generated by the process of change and how many aspects of diversity trigger strong emotional reactions. Feelings emerge when demographic changes bring you into contact with new groups, when other generations exhibit values and behaviors that you are not used to, and when cultural and language differences block communication or require you to shift your response. You can manage your reactions to such situations by understanding the threat you perceive in them and by seeing not just the losses but the gains they bring. These are key steps in becoming a "change master."

What change has diversity brought into your life? Can you identify situations that have triggered especially strong feelings in you? Are the different languages you hear from your co-workers ever a source of discomfort? Or is the introduction of new technology to the workplace sometimes unsettling? Perhaps the merger of different units and your need to report to a new manager are causing you anxiety.

Steps to Easing the Emotional Roller Coaster of Change

Being a change master gives you the framework to navigate among these and many other changes you will be experiencing. It involves identifying both the losses and the gains from change, moving toward acceptance, and finding constructive responses. Taking the following steps can help:

Step 1: Recognize the perceived losses associated with the changes and the emotional impact of those changes.

Many efforts toward implementing change fail because leaders do not, or will not, anticipate human reactions. Contrary to what most people think, people do not fear change itself. They fear the losses associated with the change. Below are some of the most common losses people resist at work.

For some the *loss of relationships,* such as when people retire or need to move to another unit, is difficult. People are not only connected to their work and organization, they are connected to other people. When you consider relationships, you may limit your thinking to people. However, individuals have relationships to other things, such as their gardens, their pets, and their hobbies. For some their creative input is like their "baby": when it is threatened, they resist the change. Victor, who has spent most of his professional life building a book collection in a college library, is shocked when top management in the organization decides to consolidate many libraries, merging different collections without any input from senior workers like Victor. He feels angry, invisible, and demoralized. He quits his job in the middle of the change, leaving the organization without one of its best performers at a time when it needs his expertise and dedication.

Other people resist the *loss of feeling competent and secure,* such as when new technologies are implemented or when a younger generation of employees enters the workplace.

For others, the *loss of their territory* brings many emotional reactions, as witnessed by fights for the best office or one of the few with windows. Sometimes the loss is of metaphoric territory, such as giving up control of a division, function, or an area of expertise.

The *loss of our identity* generates emotions, as when grown children leave home and parents feel a great vacuum—the "empty nest syndrome"—or when workers consider retirement after forty years of defining a major part of their identity through what they do.

Once you have reflected on major changes you are about to pass through, identify the perceived losses these changes might bring. Often leaders want their people to move quickly through the changes they want implemented and ignore the importance of recognizing and talking about the loss associated with change. Paradoxically, if we ignore the emotional impact of the loss inherent in major changes, we end up creating stronger resistance to them. Leaders with emotional intelligence understand the human impact of significant change and spend time talking with their people about the fears and perceived losses the change may produce.

Step 2: Replace the losses with a new perspective on opportunity.

A great way to help yourself, your employees, and your co-workers move from the past to the present and into the future is to identify a new vision, new possibilities that the change may bring about. Change, even in the most difficult situations, brings new possibilities and potential gains.

Have you considered the possible gains from a change you have undergone or are about to undergo? Checklist 3 shows many possible gains. Notice the gains your change has brought or may bring.

Focusing on the gains is one powerful way to pull out of a downward spiral of fear and doubt. It can move you to see that in most changes there are also positive outcomes that will emerge.

Another way to help you move past inherent resistance is to create a new vision of what the change might bring.

The Downsized Manager

When Peter lost his job as manager of a beauty products manufacturer due to the downsizing of his company, he feared for his financial security. He was able to move from resistance to acceptance of his situation after he created a stronger vision for his future. Peter wanted to become an entrepreneur and follow a dream of creating a chain of pastry and dessert stores. He became excited about seeing himself as an entrepreneur and started formulating a list of new skills that he needed to learn in order to make his dream more of a reality.

Checklist 3

Gains Achieved by Change

☐ Additional skills and knowledge

☐ New relationships

☐ Expanded support networks

☐ Enhanced self-esteem

☐ Increased confidence

☐ Greater empathy for and understanding of others

☐ Increased self-knowledge

☐ Greater flexibility and adaptability

☐ Deepened relationships

☐ Increased resilience

☐ More patience

☐ Increased humility

☐ Opportunity to let others feel valued and needed

☐ Greater visibility and opportunity

☐ Growth from dealing with a new, unpredictable situation

Helping people develop a new vision for themselves leads to empowerment, which helps individuals build resiliency. Managers are often in a position to help subordinates create new visions for themselves and to identify the road map that will lead them to success.

Step 3: Use the three as of change management.

When confronted with a change, three As are possible courses of action. You can do any of the following:

1. **Alter the situation** to make the change more favorable.

2. **Alter your behavior** so you can cope with the change effectively.

3. **Accept the new change** by developing a positive perspective about it.

The Christmas Holiday

Juan has worked for a textile manufacturing company for the past twenty years. Each year at Christmas he has joined his family in Mexico for two weeks, allowing him to honor both his religious values and his attachment to his extended family. The new owners of his company close their factories for three weeks each summer, leaving employees only a few days off during the holiday season. Juan comes from a culture where obeying orders is very important and challenging the boss's wishes is seen as disrespectful.

Using the three As when confronted with this change, Juan can

1. **Alter the situation** to make the change more favorable. He can ask his family members to come to the United States, shorten his traditional vacation to one week, or change his job.

2. **Alter his behavior** so he can effectively cope with the change. He can learn that assertion is welcome in this culture and begin learning the skills that will help him ask his employer to be flexible in his vacation policy.

3. **Accept the new change.** He can develop a positive perspective about it and accept his new realities and develop new traditions to celebrate with his family, use new technologies to stay connected, and develop ways to celebrate family traditions in the United States.

In Activity 9, pick a change in your own work life and practice navigating the process of change by applying the three steps just discussed.

Activity 9

Navigating the Process of Change

Write down a change in the workplace that you went through recently, that you are going through now, or that you will have to deal with in the near future.

_____

_____

_____

Go through the three steps to manage change, writing your answers below the steps.

Step 1: Recognize the perceived losses associated with the changes and the emotional impact of these losses.

_____

_____

_____

Step 2: Replace the losses with a new vision and the perspective that many opportunities might come from this change.

_____

_____

_____

Step 3: Identify which of the three As (1. Alter the situation, 2. Alter your behavior, 3. Accept the new change) you could use.

_____

_____

_____

Maps to Help You Become a Change Master

As Thomas Friedman illustrates repeatedly in his book *The World Is Flat* (New York: Farrar, Straus and Giroux, 2005), change is unrelenting in the twenty-first century. The rapidity with which it occurs and the continuous pressures it puts on us to adapt and reinvent ourselves generate intense emotions. Sometimes you value and like the changes you face—particularly those you suggest, influence, and to some degree control. Others times, however, the changes are catalysts for loss, pain, anxiety, and confusion.

By controlling your emotional reaction to change, you become your own change master, allowing you to use creative solutions to everyday challenges and to cope with minimal anger and stress. The following tips represent maps that can guide you through the process of change.

Map 1: Actions count. There is no substitute for taking action when you want change in your life. Identify an aspect of your life you would like to alter. Beginning the process, even with small steps, will create momentum.

Map 2: Change your habits. Getting more comfortable with change requires that you initiate change more frequently. Think of some of the things you do routinely; then intentionally move in new directions in those areas. Altering your habits energizes you and removes you from "autopilot." For example,

- Take a different route to work.

- Try a restaurant that features a cuisine other than the ones you prefer.

- See a movie outside the genre you typically favor.

Map 3: Use the Serenity Prayer. "Grant me the serenity to accept the things I cannot change, the courage to change the things I can, and the wisdom to know the difference" is one of the wisest pieces of advice ever offered. Identify one situation in your life you must accept and one you want to change. Write a paragraph to yourself that helps you frame the acceptance; then identify what you will change, noting the starting point.

Map 4: Travel abroad without leaving your own area. Visit an area near your own community that you rarely frequent, one that is different from your own in interesting and significant ways. Identify two positive aspects you see in that community that you would like to integrate into your own.

Map 5: Go from resister to embracer. Resisting change makes you feel like a victim, powerless over your own fate. Take back your power by identifying a change you are currently resisting. Find three ways this change can enhance your life, and identify what it would take for you to truly welcome and embrace it.

Map 6: Learn from the losses. In the face of every change, even ones you want, loss occurs. Mourn the loss, accept it, learn from it, and make it work for you. You can do this by thinking of a recent loss experienced in the context of a desired change. Label the important learning you received from it.

Getting in Charge of Your Self-Talk

*We've been taught to believe that negative equals
realistic and positive equals unrealistic.*

—SUSAN JEFFERS

Your ability to manage your emotions won't be complete until you get in charge of your self-talk. What we mean by self-talk is the internal voices or commentaries going on as you experience events and react to other people. These messages can soothe or scare you, calm or enrage you. When they are realistic, affirming, and uplifting, you can manage feelings in a healthy way. When they are negative, exaggerated, and defeating, you tend to "awfulize" the situation, which makes you feel powerless. When you make a mistake, do your voices say, "I am so stupid" or "I should have known better" or "I will never be good at this"? Perhaps they tell you, "I will do better next time" or "Although this does not come easy to me, I could get help and be better at it" or even "Now I know how to do better next time."

Taking charge of your negative self-talk is not unrealistic, Pollyannaish, rose-colored-glasses thinking. It is replacing irrational, exaggerated, and inaccurate messages with rational, realistic, and accurate ones. The power of challenging these negative inner voices and replacing them with positive ones is the essence of learning to be more resilient and optimistic—key elements of effective leaders in a diverse world.

Challenging the thoughts of fear, protection, anger, and despair is especially important in today's post-9/11 world. You are faced with people, customers, and co-workers who represent different customs, languages, values, and traditions. You could increase your fear of these differences and isolate yourself, mistrusting others and labeling them your enemies. Or you could challenge your assumptions and find ways to build bridges. In other words, you could make heaven on earth for others or produce hell. The key in choosing one over the other lies in the way you take charge of your self-talk when you are faced with differences. For example, talk with those from different ethnic groups, and ask for help in understanding their culture rather than avoiding it because of fear or embarrassment.

In her book *Feel the Fear and Do It Anyway* (San Diego: Harcourt Brace Jovanovich, 1987), Susan Jeffers provides excellent examples of how our inner voices limit our world and growth. She states that people spend too much time worrying about potential consequences when, paradoxically, 95 percent of the things they worry about never happen. Of the rest, 5 percent at most, she writes, may have negative consequences. They are rarely catastrophic. In spite of this, people act as if most consequences will be catastrophic. Jeffers describes how much time and effort people use in predicting what others may be thinking about them. The real truth is that other people are minding their own business and are overwhelmed by their own lives. Humorously, Jeffers reminds us of that we are "not the center of the universe." This awareness can free you from worrying about the judgment of others and direct your energy toward yourself, your visions, and your dreams, along with ways you can help others achieve their goals.

Identify Your Self-Talk Messages

What kind of self-talk messages are in your head when you deal with differences that are difficult, frustrating, or confusing? Becoming aware of self-talk messages is the first step. It is not as easy at it sounds. You may build many distractions and want to ignore or deny self-talk messages because they are incongruent with your self-image. Practice identifying your self-talk in Checklist 4. Check off those messages that are the most familiar to you and add others that play an important role in your life.

Checklist 4

Identify Your Self-Talk Messages

UPLIFTING AND HELPFUL MESSAGES

☐ I am up to dealing with it.

☐ I have dealt with equally or more difficult things before.

☐ I am good at what I do.

☐ I have the necessary skills and abilities.

☐ I have done the necessary preparation.

☐ This is new to me, so I may make a mistake.

☐ I am worthy of respect.

☐ I can speak up for myself.

☐ I am in charge of my life.

☐ _____

DEFEATING/HINDERING MESSAGES

☐ I am not going to be able to handle it.

☐ I will look like a fool.

☐ I will be a failure.

(continued next page)

Checklist 4 (continued)

☐ He or she will reject me.

☐ I should be able to handle it, but I can't.

☐ I should know better.

☐ I am always left out.

☐ I will be out of control.

☐ _____

Challenge Your Self-Talk Messages

Challenging self-talk voices when they are inaccurate, exaggerated, or defeating is the second step in taking charge of your self-talk. Psychologists and coaches spend a lot of time teaching leaders and workers how to refute self-talk messages when they are defeating, since they can create fear and depression. Challenging self-talk messages by replacing them with more realistic, affirming messages is key.

The Computer-Challenged Bookbinder

Hugo worked as a bookbinder, a job he held for many years. At age fifty-four he learned that his plant was closing and he would need to relocate. Most of the jobs at the new site required knowledge of computer-based programs, and none of them required his bookbinding skills. Just four years from retirement, Hugo wanted to stay with the company. So he signed up for a computer training program, but he quit after only three classes. His self-talk resulted in messages such as the following: "I am too old to master these skills." "There are a hundred people more qualified than I am." "I will never get a new job in this organization." And "I don't have what it takes."

During coaching sessions Hugo replaced these messages with more realistic and positive statements, such as the following: "I can do it. I know this is frustrating, but I have conquered similar challenges in the past." "Just be patient. Rome was not built in a day." And "There are younger applicants with better computer skills, but they lack the work experience and company wisdom I bring to the job."

In Activity 10, practice rewriting your self-talk messages by taking one of your most common negative messages and replacing it with a different, more positive one.

Activity 10

Rewriting Your Self-Talk

What are your negative self-talk messages? How can you change them?

Old negative self-talk message	New positive self-talk message

---

Gratitude as a Self-Talk Skill

Martin Seligman, author of many books on optimism and happiness, has conducted research studies that focus on the benefits of teaching individuals to replace their own negative self-talk with more optimistic perspectives. According to Seligman, gratitude is one of the most important components in a fulfilling, satisfying, and joyous life. In his classes he teaches students how to challenge negative self-talk by teaching them the "skill of being grateful."[3] According to Seligman's research, teaching people to identify and acknowledge the things that bring peace, joy, and satisfaction to their life can build self-esteem and act as a shield against many of the stressors they face every day. Therapists and executive coaches help individuals develop a more positive and optimistic perspective by having them keep daily "gratitude journals." This process of noticing the good things that happen to you and others and putting them on paper is often referred to as *mindfulness.*

Mindfulness is the ability to pay attention to your environment and inner process and be fully aware of your sensations, thoughts, and feelings. Many of the people who practice mindfulness and keep a gratitude journal report that it helps them think a little differently than they had before. They now look more closely at the "gifts" they receive, and at the benefits and opportunities that life presents them. They report feeling more energetic, empowered, and optimistic about their future.

It is important to stress that gratitude really is a choice, something you do have control over, an attitude that you can choose to have that makes life better for yourself and others. Viktor Frankl, in his extraordinary book *Man's Search for Meaning* (Boston: Beacon, 1962) reminds us that even in the worst of circumstances human beings can change their self-talk and look for meaning as a source of hope and a guide to becoming resilient. In Activity 11, practice being mindful about your life by identifying five things in your work and personal life for which you are grateful.

Activity 11

Being Grateful for Ten Things

What are you grateful for at work? In your personal life?

I am grateful for these things (at work)	I am grateful for these things (in my personal life)
1.	1.
2.	2.
3.	3.
4.	4.
5.	5.

Using Self-Talk to Help Deal with Anger

One of the most important aspects of emotional intelligence is the ability to govern feelings, particularly those related to anger. Even though anger is a normal, basic human response that everyone experiences, it is one of the toughest emotions for most people to deal with. The workplace is inundated by incidents requiring anger management. When those incidents escalate, it is usually because of the inability to deal with anger; this can often lead to the kinds of tragic situations frequently seen in the media.

Building a respectful workplace and identifying and preventing violence in it figure among the main priorities of many human resources leaders. Dealing effectively with anger is not only essential if you want to be effective and build respectful organizations, but it presents an opportunity to open communication, get to the heart of problems, and strengthen relationships. How you deal with it—whether you manage the anger or it manages you—is crucial.

Anger is an emotion triggered by unmet expectations and is, in part, a result of your internal thought process or self-talk. This means that you can use your self-talk to help you de-escalate the intensity of anger's grip. There are five areas of self-talk that may be getting you into trouble when it comes to anger.

1. **Your expectations** about the situation and the behavior of others

2. **The reasons** the situation is happening

3. **The intention** of the other person

4. **What the situation or behavior says about you**

5. **What the situation or behavior means for you**

To help manage anger, examine your self-talk in these five areas.

1. Your expectations about the situation and the behavior of others

Your values and expectations are often what govern your behavior and the expectations you have about the kind of behavior you want to see from others. In some cultures, responding to an invitation is a formal process—an acceptance to an invitation is like a contract that, if violated, will produce strong negative feelings. If you don't show up to an event that you confirmed through an RSVP, or **if you bring al**ong someone else who was not included in the original invitation, such behavior may violate strong cultural expectations. You assume that your norms and behaviors are universal and often feel angry, surprised, and annoyed at the fact that others may have different expectations about the same behavior.

Frequently employees feel angry because they expect some gesture of gratitude from their manager after a task well done, whereas their manager may have the expectation that only extraordinary achievement is recognized. How often do you feel annoyed because you expect employees to communicate only in English? Your expectations are shaped by your cultural, familial, and life experiences. It is important to understand that others are shaped by experiences that are different from yours. If you fail to take others' backgrounds into account, you take an egocentric perspective that places your norms and values above all others.

2. The reasons the situation is happening

The chances are good that the reasons the situation is happening have less to do with you than you think. Is your boss really trying to push you into leaving so he won't have to fire you? Are people not responding to your invitation because they are rude or inconsiderate, or is it because they are busy or because in their culture it is not a norm to respond formally? Are people speaking a foreign language because they want to take over or because they gravitate to what is familiar? Is your manager withholding praise because she is selfish and wants only to use you? You are limited by your own paradigms and often interpret the reasons for certain behaviors using your own "lenses." It is important to explore the reasons for a behavior by asking others and learning from their perspective.

3. The intention of the other person

Although the behavior may be upsetting, it probably wasn't intended to cause you hurt or harm. Employees are probably not talking about you when they revert to their native language, and employees probably didn't want to disrespect you by not responding to your invitation. Your boss probably does not intend to sabotage your growth, and your staff member probably doesn't intend to make a mistake that will upset your client.

Human beings personalize events and typically assume negative motivation for behaviors that create great pain and anger. It is important to withhold judgment, to avoid personalizing the intention, and to consider multiple reasons before jumping to a conclusion.

4. What the situation or behavior says about you

The chances are good that a behavior says more about the other person or group than it does about you. Does the behavior really mean that your boss doesn't trust you or have faith in your ability? Does it really mean your company doesn't value your contributions? Does it really mean your language will be lost if others speak a foreign language? Human beings are social animals. You seek admiration and approval from others, so you may often interpret the consequences of others' behavior as reflecting badly on you, which will result in a loss of admiration and praise. In turn you feel shame and anger. It is important to remember that relationships are more resilient than we think and that love, respect, and admiration are formed not necessarily by one event but by the accumulation of experiences you have had with others.

5. What the situation or behavior means for you

The consequences are not apt to be as devastating as you think. Does the behavior really mean your career is over? Does it really mean you are totally powerless to change the course of events? Does it really mean you need to swallow your rage and continue to accept the injustice of the situation? Or are the consequences less catastrophic than what you expect? You probably magnify the potentially negative impact of the consequences, so it is important to develop a more realistic perspective about events and their possible consequences.

In Activity 12, practice governing your anger. Identify a situation that causes you to be angry and refute your negative or inaccurate self-talk.

Maps to Help You Take Charge of Your Self-Talk

In today's world the ability to manage your life with so many demands and stressors and still stay optimistic is a real challenge. We often hear employees thinking and hoping for TGIF (Thank God It's Friday), hoping for Friday to come so they can relax and be happy. We find this to be sad because those with jobs spend most of their waking time at work rather than with their loved ones.

Activity 12

Governing Anger with Self-Talk

Write down a workplace situation or behavior that generates angry feelings:

_____

_____

1. Check your self-talk about the expectations you have for the situation and the behavior of others.

_____

_____

2. Check your self-talk regarding your interpretation about the reasons the situation is happening.

_____

_____

3. Check your self-talk about the intention of the other person.

_____

_____

4. Check your self-talk about what the situation or behavior says about you.

_____

_____

5. Check your self-talk about what the situation or behavior means for you.

_____

_____

The following tips will provide you with a map that will help you take charge of your self-talk and become more resilient and optimistic about life. You will be able to transform your thinking from TGIF to TGIH (Thank God I'm Here)!

Map 1: Destroy your old tapes. Identify some of the negative thoughts that pull you down. Write them out on a piece of paper; then burn or tear up the paper.

Map 2: Shrink expectations. The next time you start feeling inadequate because of unrealistic expectations, ask yourself

- What other human being could do that?

- Could anyone do more?

- What is the price of not coming through?

Map 3: Become friendly with your fears. Identify two things you may fear and the worst possible scenario stemming from their occurrence. Develop two ways of coping with them.

Map 4: Be the emissary of gratefulness. Write a letter of gratitude to someone you would like to acknowledge for something they have done or for just being part of your life. Send this person the letter.

Map 5: Call a friend. When you need a different perspective, call a friend you trust, and ask this friend to give you constructive feedback that can help you grow.

Map 6: Shift the balance. Notice how many critical rather than positive comments you make with your family and co-workers. Commit to praising more than criticizing.

The Next Steps

Our premise has been that in order to build emotional intelligence and diversity skills, you must always begin with yourself. To this end, we focused on self-awareness in Chapter 3 and skills for helping you govern your emotions in Chapter 4. In Chapter 5 we will move our focus from yourself to a broader look at others and what motivates them. In Chapter 6 we will address the social skills needed to build inclusive, respectful workplace relationships.

5

Intercultural Literacy—
Reading Others Accurately

"My team is a real United Nations! We have multiple languages and people from all parts of the world in my department." This is a common description we hear when managers talk with pride about their diverse work groups. However, we also hear managers and staff members alike express their frustrations when differences cause clashes, when confusion clouds issues, or when behaviors that people don't understand or like cause irritations. Complaints about rudeness, disrespect, and lack of professionalism and problems such as blocked communication, interrupted work flow, and stalled projects affect both morale and productivity. At times like these the United Nations comparison gives way to the Tower of Babel as a way to describe the multicultural workplace. In this Biblical tale of the building of the Tower of Babel, chaos was created and construction blocked when people were suddenly made to speak many different languages.

As you will see in this chapter, the biggest block to communication in building the Tower of Babel may have been less the different languages than people's inability to correctly interpret one another's behavior and extend empathy toward one another. Had individuals been able to connect emotionally and show understanding, the language differences could have been bridged.

Because of the higher risk of misunderstanding, unintended offense, or unwarranted conflict that can occur in multicultural environments, Intercultural Literacy is critical. To be successful in today's diverse workplace, you need to be able to get along with people who may be very different from you. Getting along requires three skills. First, you need the tools to read others accurately so you can correctly decode their behavior and not misinterpret it. Second, you need the ability to see the potential advantages and disadvantages in others' ways so you can avoid making judgments that can alienate others. Third, you need empathy, which enables you to develop meaningful connections with others no matter how different they may be. These are the skills of Intercultural Literacy.

Few people were born with Intercultural Literacy skills, and your knee-jerk responses to differences, especially ones you don't like or understand, may not be helping you be successful. Have you ever wondered why someone does something that seems odd or doesn't make sense to you? Why did that employee nod and say he understood when he didn't? Why does your co-worker always stand too close to you? Why does your client get so angry when you are a little late? Why does your boss expect you to make an appointment to see him instead of just meeting with you when you stop by? The answers may be cultural. In today's multicultural world, understanding the meaning underlying the behaviors of others is key to your effectiveness on the job. Intercultural Literacy is about being able to decode a wide variety of behaviors so you can deal with them effectively, and has three components.

Components of Intercultural Literacy

▦ Understanding the cultural whys behind behavior

▦ Seeing the upsides and downsides of all cultural norms

▦ Transcending your own perspective and showing empathy

Understanding the Cultural Whys Behind Behavior

We see what is behind our eyes.

—CHINESE PROVERB

When you think of culture, do art museums, opera, and classical music come to mind? Well, these are one part of culture, the aesthetic products of a society.

However, culture is about more than highbrow pursuits. It has an even more powerful and pervasive impact. This everyday part involves the norms, rules, and values that teach people how to interact and how to interpret the behavior of others. Have you ever

- Been surprised when a staff member dissolved in tears and seemed deeply humiliated when you gave what you would consider objective, nonaccusing feedback?

- Been put off by a soft handshake?

- Been shocked when someone misinterpreted your actions, accusing you of sexist or racist behavior when you had no such intent?

- Been irritated by someone's roundabout, unclear explanation and wished they would just get to the point?

If you have faced any of these situations, you were probably experiencing cultural differences. While you may have been perplexed or irritated, you might not have known you lacked cultural knowledge and that you had misinterpreted a behavior. Or if you were aware that cultural differences were operating, you may not have known enough about them to understand what was going on.

Understanding the wide range of cultural behaviors and preferences and the meanings that underlie them is a critical part of emotional intelligence in diverse environments. Having knowledge about the whys behind behaviors helps you avoid the misunderstandings that can take place when you interpret others' actions solely through your own cultural lens. Seeing a wider range of possible reasons for a particular behavior allows you to investigate beyond your initial reaction so you can read the other person more accurately and then respond more appropriately.

We once worked with a manager who had a question about some of the engineers he supervised. He said that whenever he explained a new process or discussed a new project, a group of his team members who were from Taiwan would smile and laugh. It seemed to him like an odd reaction, and his only explanation was that these engineers were snickering and laughing at him. While he had much respect for these team members and was pleased with the quality of their work, this behavior bothered him. Once he gained some cultural knowledge and learned that laughter and smiling can be a sign of embarrassment and confusion in parts of Asia, he had a different reaction. Suddenly it made sense. With this information, not only did he reinterpret the meaning of their behavior and reduce his own irritation, but he could also respond more appropriately and productively when it happened. This is why understanding the cultural whys behind behavior can be so critical.

Behavioral/Cultural Software

One way to understand culture is to see it as "behavioral software," which is what Geert Hofstede, noted interculturalist and author, calls it.[1] Culture, like software, is a set of operating rules for how to solve problems; in the case of cultural software, it is rules to help relate to others and survive in social settings. Culture gives each person the rules for interacting, from how to address a boss, respond at a meeting, and show gratitude to how to resolve conflict, disagree, and give feedback. Beyond teaching you how to behave, your cultural software also teaches you how to interpret the rules of others. For example, do you see the person who arrives late as inconsiderate, disorganized, or operating with a different time orientation? Do you assume the person who does not make eye contact is deceitful, lacking confidence, or respectful? Do you view the person who tells a story in a circular fashion as disorganized because he doesn't get to the point, or as a powerful communicator who makes his point in an indirect way? How you interpret the behavior will depend on your cultural software.

Like fish in water, individuals aren't usually aware of their cultural programming until they bump up against different cultural software programs. The first place to start in understanding different cultural software is to become more aware of your own. On Checklist 5, check off any of the rules that are part of your software. Think about how they influence how you act and what you expect from others.

As you look at some of the rules you checked, think about how they guide your behavior and form some of your expectations of others. Consider how many of your rules are compatible with the rules of your co-workers, bosses, and employees. Also reflect on which of their rules are different from yours and which are irritating for you. To help yourself learn about the software of others, make a list of the five people with whom you work most closely, and

---

Checklist 5

Your Cultural Software

- ☐ Say what's on your mind.
- ☐ Never cause loss of face.
- ☐ Show respect and deference to elders.
- ☐ Be punctual.
- ☐ Stay until the work is done.
- ☐ Family comes first.
- ☐ Honesty is the best policy.
- ☐ Be generous.
- ☐ Stand up for what's right.
- ☐ Don't make waves.
- ☐ Be proud of who you are.
- ☐ Be humble and don't toot your own horn.
- ☐ Save for the future.
- ☐ Respect your elders.

- ☐ Life is short, so live fully now.
- ☐ Ask for forgiveness rather than permission.
- ☐ Take risks.
- ☐ Think before you speak.
- ☐ Be direct in dealing with problems and conflicts.
- ☐ Always go the extra mile.
- ☐ Make people feel welcome.
- ☐ Winning is everything.
- ☐ Money isn't everything.
- ☐ What you give away comes back to you.
- ☐ Actions speak louder than words.
- ☐ _____

---

jot down some of the rules of their cultural software. Then consider your reactions to their rules. Finally, make a commitment to spend some time individually with these people and discuss your rules and theirs.

Interpreting Others' Behavior

Not only do the rules of your cultural software direct your behavior, but they give you the framework for interpreting the behavior of others. For example, if you believe that promptness is a virtue, you might see latecomers as disrespectful, lazy, rude, or disorganized. However, with a higher level of Intercultural Literacy you might find out that the person has a more relaxed sense of time, cares more about what gets done than when, and sees your promptness as rigid and bureaucratic. Figure 4 shows what happens when you experience another's behavior.

You *observe* a behavior; for example, you are confronted with a group speaking in a language you don't understand. You decode the behavior: for example, you think they are talking about you. Then you *react* with both feelings and actions; for example, you may feel hurt and walk away or you may get angry and loudly ask, "So what's the big secret?" Usually the decoding is what gets you in trouble, because when it is incorrect, it leads you to behave in counterproductive ways. When you investigate, you may find other meanings for the behavior. In this case, perhaps they had a question about a work project and found it easier and more accurate to be able to speak in their first language. Maybe the subject was a personal one that they wanted to keep private. Or maybe you were right, and they were talking about you. The key to reacting appropriately is to get additional information so you can more accurately decode the meaning of the behavior.

Once you question your assumptions and find out the whys behind behaviors, the cultural software of others is apt to be less irritating to you. As you think of some of the most difficult behaviors you deal with, see if you can find

Figure 4: Interpreting Behavior

more about the whys behind them. Perhaps the staff member who doesn't give feedback in the meeting isn't just lacking in ideas but values harmony, so he doesn't want to make waves by giving input that might be contrary. You might consider other ways to get his input. Perhaps the team member who speaks up, gives opinions, and volunteers for projects does so because she is more individualistic and prizes initiative and is not being just a grandstander. You might see if you can reassess your judgment and appreciate the value she brings to the team. Once you see behaviors in their cultural contexts, without judgment, you will find it easier to come up with ways to work more effectively with others.

Common Reactions to Other Cultural Norms

It's not unusual to question or react critically to a cultural norm different from your own. Following are some common reactions and a more in-depth look at those issues.

What about "When in Rome, do as the Romans do?"

You might be wondering why this advice isn't being followed. Anyone who has come into a new culture, whether it's a new country, new organization, or new team, knows that some adaptation is required. In order to survive, the newcomer needs to make some adjustments to the existing rules, practices, and norms. However, "Rome" is also changing. In today's workplaces, the existing norms and rules are evolving, and adaptation needs to be a two-way street. Requiring newcomers to make all the adjusting keeps the organization from using and benefiting from the different methods and ideas that new entrants might bring. As one employee said, "They hired me for my differences; then once I got here they started chopping off my corners."

Why do I have to learn about them?
They're in my country or organization now.

Learning about the culture of others is not an altruistic move. Knowing more about the whys behind their behavior helps you by making your job easier and enabling you to be more effective. When you misunderstand someone's behavior and act on your misinterpretation, you'll generally do things that don't get your needs or objectives met. When you do understand, you can use that knowledge to help you find a better approach. If, for example, you think that team members' lack of verbal participation and input at staff meetings means that they have no ideas to add, or that they are unmotivated or lacking in intelligence, you may cease seeking any contributions from them and cheat yourself out of the benefit of their perspectives. However, if you realize that their lack of verbal participation may be because they do not want to stand out from the group, are too shy to speak out, or feel that it is inappropriate for a subordinate to make suggestions to the boss, you might take a different approach. You could have team members work in small groups to generate suggestions and then present them to the entire team, or you might meet with these staff members individually to hear their views. Understanding more about them helps you in the end.

But I'm right and they're wrong.

You may be right; however, you need to be both right and effective. It will be hard for you to gain the commitment and support of others if you maintain a rigid, self-righteous adherence to being right. Although there are some objective, provable right answers (water boils at 212 degrees at sea level, and there are thirty-six inches in a yard), many of the issues you deal with at work have more than one right answer. If you keep your focus on the end objective, you will find it easier to accept different ways of getting there. Does it matter whether someone says yes or no as long as you know whether the person understands and can perform the task? Does it matter if someone works on projects at the office or at home as long as the person comes through and completes them?

One senior manager was frustrated when he saw that his company had gone with a right answer that was not effective. It was time to replace employees' computers with newer, updated models. To save $200 a person, the company opted for desktop computers rather than laptops. In doing so it missed an opportunity with many of the younger staff, who would have taken their laptops home and worked many extra hours on company projects. In its attempt to be thrifty, the organization was right but not effective, because it had not considered the cultural software of a large group of its employees.

The next section will help you gain knowledge about some of the main cultural differences influencing interactions in your workplace.

Understanding the Range of Cultural Norms

Cultures around the world vary in many respects. Read the following important variations that affect the work environment and influence interactions and relationships on the job, then take the quiz on pages 108–110.

1. Individualistic ◄————► Collectivistic

"It's a free country" and "Do your own thing" are hallmarks of the individualistic orientation common in the United States. Seeing yourself as an individual performer and wanting to be rewarded on that basis are part of this orientation. At the other end of the continuum, you would have a more collectivistic orientation if you saw yourself as a group member first and had a "One for all, all for one," outlook. Staff members from this orientation might have a difficult time talking about their individual accomplishments or contributions and might not want to be singled out for public praise. On the other hand, those who are more individualistic might bristle at all the team projects and group work and prefer to work on their own.

2. Monochronic ◄————► Polychronic

Another difference among cultures and the individuals within them has to do with how people think about and use time. "The early bird catches the worm" and "Time is money" represent a monochronic orientation in which time is viewed as a commodity to be used to accomplish tasks. It is divided into segments—spent, saved, and scheduled. At the other end of this range is a polychronic sense of time in which many things can go on at once and time is used for relationships and enjoyment as well as for tasks. The monochronic individual would expect the meeting to begin and end at the times indicated on the memo and would undoubtedly be irritated at latecomers and sessions that go overtime. The polychronic individual would place less emphasis on the clock, wanting the meeting to begin when the necessary people are there and end when what needs to get done is accomplished.

3. Hierarchical ⟵⟶ Egalitarian

Social order brings another difference among cultures. "Leave your stripes at the door" attitudes, team-run plants, and participative management represent an egalitarian orientation. For those with a hierarchical perspective, the chain of command is seen as helpful in providing order and a sense of place and in letting people know where the responsibility lies. Employees or co-workers from this orientation might find it difficult to disagree with a boss, give input at a meeting, or confront someone in a higher position. On the other hand, someone from a more egalitarian orientation would expect to be able to call an executive directly, take an active role in multilevel problem solving, and be on a first-name basis with executives. For example, a young assembly-line worker from Mexico refused a promotion to supervisor. When asked why he didn't want the management position, he explained that he and his work group had all come from the same village, and there were a number of older men in the group. Being a supervisor would require him to give orders to older men. Coming from a culture that shows deference to age, he felt doing this would be wrong.

4. Task ⟵⟶ Relationship

Although being focused on both getting the job done and attending to relationships are necessary, cultures differ in their priorities regarding these two perspectives. Do you build relationships by working shoulder-to-shoulder with someone on a project, or do you find that building relationships first helps you get the work done more effectively? Task-oriented individuals might start the meeting with an agenda and objectives, while relationship-oriented people might start with a personal check-in and schmooze time. Both of these perspectives are essential to productivity and effectiveness. However, those who are task oriented might be critical of what they consider time wasted in socializing, and those who are relationship oriented might be put off by the lack of connection and interpersonal ties with co-workers. Balancing these two perspectives and seeing the value in each are key.

5. Differences ⟵⟶ Harmony

Another culturally influenced factor is how people deal with conflict. In some cultures the preservation of harmony in relationships is prized. Keeping relations smooth and the waters calm is of prime importance. In other cultures, tackling differences is seen as the best way to work through issues and conflicts. Speaking up and openly confronting differences is necessary for resolution and is not meant to be disruptive. While those who seek harmony would not want to do anything that would disturb the peace, those who raise differences don't want to avoid dealing with problems.

These preferences became evident in one department where staff members nearly came to blows when a problem escalated because of cultural differences in this dimension. One employee, an African American woman who came from a background that taught her to confront issues directly in order to deal with them, approached her co-worker and announced the problem. Her colleague from the Philippines was taken aback. Because her upbringing had taught her to keep relationships harmonious and not cause disruption, her response was to back away from her colleague and try to avoid confrontation. Her co-worker, on the other hand, didn't understand the reaction and kept pursuing her, talking about their differences and how this conflict needed to be resolved in order to get their work done. Finally, the staff member from the Philippines stopped in her tracks and said, "If you take one step closer to me, I'm going to hit you." Both of them went to human resources and complained about being physically threatened. Had they better understood each other's cultural software in this dimension, perhaps this confrontation could have been prevented. Again, valuing both ends of the continuum is essential for teamwork and effectiveness.

6. Low context ⟵——————⟶ High context

How to communicate is still another variation in cultural norms. In low-context cultures, communication is direct; it is the sender's responsibility to explain, and the meaning is carried explicitly in the words. In high-context cultures the meaning is in the context around the words—body language, tone, and the relationship of the communicators. In this view it is up to the listener to infer the meaning. "Put your cards on the table," "Tell it like it is," and "Get to the point" represent the direct, explicit preference of low-context cultures. An employee from a low-context background would generally state the facts, make a presentation with bulleted points, and give explicit directions. One from a high-context culture might tell a story to make a point and give a broad outline rather than a list of points.

The Absent Guests

Cultural differences caused some discomfort when a company owner hosted a holiday party at a hotel at a year-end celebration to show appreciation to his employees. When few of his immigrant workers attended, though most had indicated they would, he felt first hurt and then angry. When he investigated, he found out some of the reasons why. The workers said they felt awkward about going to a social event at a fancy hotel, their wives were worried that they didn't have appropriate clothes, and they couldn't imagine a holiday party without their children. When asked why they didn't just say they wouldn't attend, they said that they could not directly refuse an invitation that they knew was meant as a gift to them. At the same time, they could not come because of the discomfort in attending. Being from a high-context culture, they did not communicate this explicitly and thought that these factors would be understood. The owner learned from this experience and the following year hosted a well-attended family picnic and barbecue for the holiday celebration.

Activity 13

Understanding Your Cultural Orientation

Take the quiz below to better understand your own cultural orientation in these six dimensions. For each dimension, circle two statements that best describe you at work.

1. Individualistic/Collectivistic (Circle two)

    a. I work best independently and see myself as an individual contributor first. (I)

    b. I work best in a group or team and see myself as part of the group first. (C)

    c. I prefer to be rated on my own individual performance and accomplishment. (I)

    d. I prefer to be rated on the team's performance and accomplishment. (C)

Activity 13 (continued)

2. **Mon**och**r**onic/Polychronic (Circle two)

   a. I like to be on time and expect the same of others. (M)

   b. I like to start a meeting when the right people are there and end when the purpose of the meeting has been accomplished. (P)

   c. Deadlines, schedules, and timelines are sacred to me. (M)

   d. Deadlines, schedules, and timelines are negotiable for me. (P)

3. **Hierarchical/Egalitarian (Circle two)**

   a. I work best when there is a clear rank and a chain of command. (H)

   b. I work best with little emphasis on titles and status. (E)

   c. I like a formal tone and respect for set procedures. (H)

   d. I like an informal tone and will challenge procedures that get in my way. (E)

4. **Task/Relationship (Circle two)**

   a. I prefer to focus on getting the job done and get impatient with socializing. (T)

   b. I value time spent in building relationships and work better with people when I get to know them. (R)

   c. I like to start the meeting with an agenda to keep us on track. (T)

   d. I like to start the meeting with a personal check-in to connect us. (R)

5. **Differences/Harmony (Circle two)**

   a. I directly address differences when there is an issue so the problem can be solved. (D)

   b. I deal with differences indirectly behind the scenes to avoid causing upset. (H)

   c. I do not like to ignore a problem to avoid conflict. (D)

   d. I do not like to bring up a problem and cause tension or hurt feelings. (H)

6. **Low Context/High Context (Circle two)**

   a. I prefer direct, specific, and explicit verbal communication. (LC)

   b. I prefer general, open-ended communication and depend on nonverbal cues. (HC)

   c. I explain with bulleted points and specific directions. (LC)

   d. I explain with stories and metaphors. (HC)

(continued next page)

Activity 13 (continued)

Now that you have selected two statements in each set, look at the letters in parentheses that follow the statements. These indicate which orientation your selected statement relates to. I means that your answer relates to an individualistic orientation while C means it connects to a collectivistic one. You may see a clear indication of your orientation in each dimension if both your selections relate to the same orientation. However, you may find that the two statements you selected relate to different orientations. This result tells you that you are balanced and operate using elements of both orientations.

Once you have taken the quiz and interpreted your results, you know more about your cultural orientation. Now consider the following questions to see how your cultural software plays out on the job.

1. How does your orientation influence your feelings and behavior at work?

For example, if you are more monochronic, you may get frustrated at meetings that don't start on time. If you are more task oriented, you may see that you question the work ethic of relationship-oriented people and avoid bringing them onto your team.

2. How does your orientation help and hinder you?

Maybe you see that your low-context directness in communicating helps reduce confusion. On the other hand, your desire for harmony prevents you from giving the honest feedback and having the difficult conversations that are needed to help an employee grow.

3. Which orientations are most difficult for you to deal with in others, and how do you deal with them?

Being interculturally literate involves not only understanding the software of others but being able to work effectively with a wide range of orientations. For example, if you get irritated with collectivists who don't claim their individual accomplishments, you may find that you give them poorer performance ratings or discount them in hiring interviews.

4. How can you use your knowledge of culture to find the
   value that those with different orientations bring to the team?

The harmonizer who doesn't directly confront conflict may not be an avoider but may be helping the team focus on common ground. The relationship-oriented employee may not be just a social butterfly but a unifier who creates the interpersonal ties that hold the team together.

Steps to Understanding the Cultural Software of Others

Understanding the major differences in cultural orientation plays an important part in figuring out the whys behind behavior. You can also help yourself find out more about the whys behind behaviors that are perplexing, irritating, or just different by taking the following four steps.

1. Keep in mind that the behavior makes sense to the other person.

A basic fact of human behavior is that no one does anything that doesn't make sense to him or her. This fact is hard to grasp when the person's behavior makes you scratch your head and wonder what he or she was thinking that led to a particular action. Understanding that the behavior makes sense to the individual doesn't mean that you need to accept or approve of the behavior. What it does mean is that you have more clues to help you deal with it more effectively and to reduce the irritation that may be blocking your thinking. One employee from Mexico would take the day off to drive his wife to her doctor's appointment, even though she had a car and could drive. The employee's manager was frustrated and angry. But once he learned that the employee did this because his wife was going through difficult treatments and the employee felt it was his duty as head of the family to take care of her, the manager cooled off and was able to find some workable solutions to the problem.

2. Acknowledge your own assumptions about what the behavior means to you.

When someone's behavior triggers an emotional response, such as frustration, confusion, or discomfort in you, stop and ask yourself what the action means to you. It is your interpretation that is causing the emotional reaction, not the other person's behavior, so consciously acknowledging the assumptions that are triggering feelings in you is key. You might think that downcast eyes signal deceit or lack of confidence. You might assume that nods and yes responses indicate agreement and understanding. Or you might interpret the direct confrontational style of questioning as hostility and resistance. Admitting these assumptions is a necessary step in moderating your emotional response and in understanding the individual.

3. Ask yourself what the behavior might mean to the other person.

Once you admit your own assumptions, you then need to go to the next step. Because each person has a different cultural software program, the behavior you find annoying may have an entirely different meaning to the person doing it. The downcast eyes may be showing respect and deference to you because of your status or age rather than deceit or lack of confidence. The nods and yes responses may indicate a desire to be harmonious and supportive rather than showing agreement and understanding. The confrontational questioning may be a sincere desire to clarify and understand rather than to resist.

4. Ask the person in question, or another individual from that same background, to help you understand the behavior.

Ultimately you need to find out what the behavior means to the person doing it. Sometimes the best way to clarify the meaning is to go to directly to the individual. One African American staff member became enraged at her chief executive officer's (CEO's) continual memos and questions about racial issues. Her boss noticed her reaction and asked her about it. She explained that her strong emotional response stemmed from the fact that affirmative action and equal employment opportunity issues were not a responsibility of her job and that she was not the spokesperson for all African Americans. She also added that the CEO never came to her with questions about training and development, which was her area of responsibility. To her it looked as though the only thing the CEO saw in her was her race, not her competence and professional skill. In this case, by going directly to the individual involved, the manager got a clearer understanding of the situation, an understanding she used to give helpful feedback to the CEO.

At times when emotions run high, though, going directly to the individual may not be effective. Then it is useful to find a "cultural informer," someone who can help you understand different cultural software. An executive took this approach when she was deeply hurt by being labeled racist by the staff of a poorly managed and failing business unit she had been sent to reorganize in a turnaround project. When she ran into problems, she called in a professional to help untangle the situation and overcome the staff's resistance to her. With the help of the diversity consultant, who served as a cultural informer, she learned more about the cultural norms and preferences of her mostly Filipino staff, and she gained an understanding of how critical personal relationships were to them. More importantly, she learned that they were resisting the new policies and procedures not because they wanted to be difficult and block change but because she had not made any attempt to build interpersonal connections and trust with them first. They saw her strong task orientation as cold and uncaring, and they closed ranks against her. They were acting out the old dictum "I don't care how much you know until I know how much you care." Having this cultural information gave her the keys to finding approaches that helped solve this impasse and get the cooperation and follow-through she needed to get this business unit back on its feet.

Maps to Help You Learn More About Other Cultural Norms

These tips can serve as your maps, guiding you in learning more about other cultures.

Map 1: Take an armchair trip. Experience other cultures through films or books. Each month see a film or read a book about another culture. Films such as *Monsoon Wedding, Real Women Have Curves,* and *My Big Fat Greek Wedding,* and books such as *Three Cups of Tea, The Bookseller of Kabul,* and *The Joy Luck Club* are examples of these. Notice the similarities and the differences between the cultures portrayed and your own. Seek new insights and understandings as you enjoy the experience of being a virtual visitor in another culture.

Map 2: Recruit a culture coach. Seek out a colleague or friend who is from another background to be your coach, who can teach you about his or her culture and explain some of its most important rules, customs, and values.

Map 3: Tune in to the clues. Cultural norms and values show themselves in behaviors and situations all the time. Tune in to the clues that let you know what is preferred or expected. For example, the fact that your employee is embarrassed by public praise, that your co-worker stiffens when you hug him, or that your boss looks at her watch when you stop by her office to chat are all clues to their cultural software. Think of a couple of people whose behavior is difficult for you and make a commitment to tune in to the clues they are giving you.

Map 4: Go to the source. Ask the person for information directly in a nonaccusing way, showing a sincere desire to understand. "I notice you rarely volunteer for project presentations. I was wondering why." "You have wonderful ideas, but you don't offer suggestions in our brainstorming sessions. Can you help me understand why?" By asking, you may find that the person who doesn't volunteer to give presentations is shy, self-conscious about his accent, or doesn't want to be singled out from the group. You might learn that the person who doesn't participate in brainstorming is a more reflective thinker who needs more time to consider ideas and would appreciate advance notice about the topics on the agenda. Or you may find out that the person is from a hierarchical culture and thinks that making suggestions to the boss is disrespectful and inappropriate.

Map 5: Seek out resources. When you need to gain knowledge about a particular culture and its norms and values, go to books and online resources for help. Books such as *Kiss, Bow, or Shake Hands; Straight Talk about Gays in the Workplace; Good Neighbors: Communicating with the Mexicans,* and books published by Intercultural Press (www.interculturalpress.com) are examples of the kinds of publications that can be helpful in giving you culture-specific information. Online resources such as GlobeSmart (www.globesmart.com) can provide similar assistance. Just make sure that the source you go to gives you information about the cultural orientations and values that influence workplace behavior and is not a travel guide to the sights and geography of the country. If your team is dealing with cross-cultural difficulties, another resource, Cultural Detective (www.culturaldetective.com) is a helpful training tool to help team members develop a greater understanding and tolerance of cultural differences that are affecting team performance.

Seeing the Upsides and Downsides of All Cultural Norms

Nothing is either good or bad but thinking makes it so.
—SHAKESPEARE

It is normal, natural, and often most comfortable to approach cultural differences from an ethnocentric perspective, seeing your own way as right or superior. Moderating that judgment and understanding that all cultural norms have both upsides and downsides is generally not an automatic response, yet it is a key element of Intercultural Literacy because it helps you

- Have more patience and tolerance for different values and beliefs
- Be more open to cultivating different points of view
- Make fewer judgments and negative interpretations about why others do what they do
- Ask questions without judging so you can learn more
- Remain objective in the face of differences that are difficult to deal with
- Be more flexible with your own perspective
- Have more possible responses in your repertoire
- Have greater insight into the impact of your software on others

All of these elements help reduce the chance for feelings to heat up, and as a result it is possible for you to respond in more effective ways, no matter how difficult the behavior you encounter.

Culture is both pervasive and subtle at the same time. It affects everything you and others do, yet it is so much a part of who you are that it is usually automatic, and you probably don't think much about it. It is gained mostly through osmosis, so it is often unconscious, and most people aren't aware of the cultural rules that are influencing their actions. It's just the way things are, and it seems like the right way. You usually notice it when you run into people who do things differently, and when that happens, you might feel confused, irritated, uncomfortable, threatened, or inadequate.

When you do experience cultural differences, the typical reaction is rarely curiosity. More often, it is judgment, and you probably see the behavior of others as wrong, undesirable, or deficient. Statements like "I can't trust her. She never looks me in the eye" and "He's a very aggressive person who always invades my space. He stands way too close" are not uncommon when people don't understand behaviors that underlie cultural norms. You may be uncomfortable if a person from the Middle East stands much closer to you than you like, but once you know that the reason for the behavior lies in a difference in cultural norms, you might be able to reconsider your response and see the behavior as a way to feel connected rather than to be aggressive.

Seeing the benefits and limitations of all norms requires two steps. The first is to understand your own behavior and assess how it might look from another culture's perspective. For example, American individualism encourages initiative, independence, and gumption, which can lead to efficiency, problem solving, and breakthroughs. However, from a more group-oriented, collectivist perspective, these same behaviors can also be seen as selfish, domineering, isolating, or uncooperative.

Sometimes it is comical to see ourselves through the eyes of others. In one Korean-owned bank where employees were a mix of U.S. and Korean born, staff found this out at a cultural diversity training. At first talking about the differences they noticed in one another's culture was uncomfortable. However, they finally began to open up. In a conversation about table manners, one of the U.S.-born staff finally asked, "Why do you chew with your mouth open?" Her Korea-born co-worker responded with, "Why do you blow your nose at the table?" Both were letting the other know how they saw the other's behavior, and both sides learned that cultural judgments go two ways. Although you may find fault in other people's cultural practices, they may find fault in yours as well.

The second step you need to master is the ability to find the strength and good news in norms of others, especially ones that you don't like. For example, if an applicant from Central America or China comes to a job interview and greets you with a soft handshake, your Intercultural Literacy will keep you from dismissing this person as a timid and underconfident job applicant.

Rather, you will be able to entertain the possibility that the handshake is culturally influenced, and its purpose is to make connection and extend warmth.

Because like most people you probably see your norms and preferences as right, it is usually difficult to see the upsides of those of others, especially the norms and preferences you don't like. Take a look at the norms in Checklist 6 and check off a few that are difficult for you.

Once you've selected a few cultural norms that are difficult or undesirable for you, try to figure out the upside of those behaviors, listing a few benefits each brings.

Maps to Help You See and Value Different Perspectives

Managing emotions well requires both reframing of your own cultural norms to see how they might seem less desirable to others and seeing behaviors of others in an open, nonjudgmental way. Use the following maps to develop those abilities.

Map 1: Imagine why the other person thinks or behaves as he or she does. What positive motivation would the person have for doing this? Imagine yourself in the person's context or situation and try to come up with the reasons for his or her choices.

Map 2: Develop the habit of asking yourself a standard question. When you feel your viewpoint narrowing or find yourself reacting negatively to a behavior you don't like, ask questions such as "What is the upside of this behavior?" " How might this behavior help?" or "What value does this behavior bring to the team?"

Map 3: Put your judgments aside as you genuinely search for answers. Keep the judgment out of both your words and your nonverbal reactions, such as your tone and facial expressions. Sometimes judgments are disguised as questions, so make sure your question is a sincere request for information rather than a statement of judgment. "Why didn't you do it this way?" is not a real question but rather a statement.

Map 4: Temporarily take an opposition position. Write down why that behavior or choice makes sense and can be beneficial. Work with this until you can really come up with ways the action or behavior adds value.

Checklist 6

Cultural Norms and Preferences

☐ Speaking a language that some in the workplace cannot understand

☐ Coming late to meetings and appointments

☐ Withholding ideas and not participating in discussions

☐ Not giving clear, direct feedback

☐ Communicating vaguely and ambiguously

☐ Speaking loudly in a gruff, off-putting way

☐ Putting duty to family before work

☐ Never staying late with the team

☐ Not adapting to the norms of the team or organization

☐ Working alone and not being a team player

☐ Using relationships to get ahead

☐ Giving gifts to the boss

☐ Not giving praise or positive feedback

☐ Avoiding conflict and difficult conversations

☐ Giving long and rambling explanations

☐ Talking about family issues at work

☐ _____

Map 5: Look at your own behavior from a different perspective. Think of some of your favorite, most comfortable ways of doing things. Maybe you always get to meetings early, like to send out agendas ahead of time, or communicate mostly by e-mail. First identify the benefits of your way of doing things. After all, you wouldn't be doing something if it was not helpful. Then identify the drawbacks. For example, maybe being the first one at the meeting creates stress for you, makes you impatient with others who come later, or causes those who aren't on time to distance themselves from you because of what they perceive as your disapproval. Maybe your advance agendas prevent others from giving input and make them feel that outcomes are predetermined. Or perhaps your e-mails overwhelm others with too much information or keep them from connecting with you on a more informal basis. If you are having difficulty seeing the downsides of your preferences, try to view yourself from the perspective of someone who does not behave as you do. Seeing that your norms and preferences have potential negative sides is as important as seeing that the ways of others have positive sides.

Map 6: Spend time with people whose perspectives are different from yours. It is a natural human response to seek out and feel more comfortable with others who see things your way. Their views validate yours, and you probably feel supported by their agreement. Those who see things differently may be challenging, yet you often need their buy-in and cooperation. One newly appointed judge found out how beneficial it could be to spend time with her colleagues who saw and did things differently. As the first and only female judge on one of the circuits of the U.S. Court of Appeals, she was the new person and needed to understand and be able to work effectively with her male colleagues on the bench. At first she felt like an outsider. However, once she noticed that her fellow judges spent their lunch hour each day playing dominoes, she found a path to connection. She learned dominoes and began to join them for games each day. Not only did she develop relationships with them and move from outsider to insider, she learned how they thought. This knowledge of how they strategized helped her in getting them to buy her ideas and decisions, because she could explain and position them in ways that the other judges could understand and accept.

Transcending Your Own Perspective and Showing Empathy

Be not disturbed at being misunderstood.
Be disturbed at not understanding.
—CHINESE PROVERB

Intercultural Literacy requires one more skill—empathy, the ability to walk in another's shoes. Empathy is one of the most important skills that emotionally intelligent individuals display. It is especially critical in a diverse environment, because where there are multiple differences, there is less initial common ground and greater need for connection. Empathy is where the heart and the mind interact to make powerful connections between people. The majority of communication is nonverbal, and part of the reason that individuals can be in tune with one another in the most fundamental way, even if they speak different languages, is that they are able to understand the feelings beneath the words.

Empathy is more than a skill. It is an attitude, an approach that shows genuine caring. It helps you transcend your focus on yourself and put your attention on the other person. In essence, it is listening with your heart. This kind of connection is not just something that feels good. It is essential to productive interactions and satisfying relationships, on the job and off. When a real connection is felt, most differences can be bridged and most problems can be solved. Empathy does more than demonstrate an understanding of another's feelings, connect you to others, and deepen the communication. It is a powerful tool to deal with emotionally charged situations because it also helps calm upset individuals, overcome resistance, and avoid arguments.

Steps to Developing Empathy

The good news is that empathy can be learned. It requires you to shift your perspective to one that reflects a willingness to be genuinely receptive to another person. It challenges you to assume a position of curiosity to fully understand the situation at hand by trying to place yourself in the other person's reality. Empathy entails the following four specific steps.

1. Suspend judgment.

To feel and demonstrate empathy, you must first suspend judgment and take a position of curiosity to try to fully understand the situation at hand. Tell yourself, "I'm genuinely interested in understanding this situation." Rather than judging an employee who continues to break a rule, for example, step back and open your mind to the many factors that may be involved. One director took this step and found that it made all the difference in dealing with a problem with one of her staff members. The staff member, a night shift employee, continued to use the telephone at work to make personal calls, even though this was against company policy. She was warned, counseled, and told that she was putting her job at risk, but she continued to make calls. The immediate supervisor was at her wit's end and as a last resort called in the director to help. Instead of judging the staff member, the director approached her with real curiosity. She said, "You are a competent employee and a smart woman, yet you continue to do something that is going to get you fired. What is going on?" The staff member finally broke down and explained that she did not have child care for her three young children and was calling home to check on them. Once the two of them got to the bottom of the issue, they were able to solve the problem by getting her the child care help she needed. This result would not have been achieved without the director's caring, nonjudgmental curiosity.

2. Temporarily abandon your perspective.

This step requires that you try to walk in the other person's shoes. Put yourself in the other person's position. How might the situation look from the other person's perspective? What might it feel like? What options might you see from this vantage point? One way to do this is to pretend to be this person for a few minutes and explain the situation and the options as they might look to you in that role. Another is to give people the opportunity though cross-training, job rotation, or visits to be in the other's spot. Remember, the individual is doing what seems right and best from his or her perspective.

One manager of a large construction firm found a way to institutionalize this step, and the method did wonders in resolving a group-on-group conflict that was costing the organization money and getting in the way of productivity. The accounts payable staff, who took care of paying the travel reimbursements for the job site superintendents, were in a confrontation with the field staff, and the superintendents were angry that their reimbursements were months behind. Tempers flared, and the situation continued to escalate. The chief architect in charge saw the problem and realized that neither group understood the other's reality. First, he tried walking in the shoes of the accounts payable staff and thought about what they might be experiencing. When he did this, he realized that they worked in cubicles with no windows in the basement of the headquarters building, and they had virtually no discretionary time and rarely got any perks in their jobs. When they received the expense reports from the field, they saw expensive restaurant receipts for lavish lunches and airline flights around the country. Not surprisingly, they were resentful at what they viewed as the glamour and excitement of the life on the job site. They responded by nitpicking details, sending forms back to be redone and generally slowing down the process. The superintendents, on the other hand, irritated at having to wait months to get their money back, viewed the office staff as rigid bureaucrats throwing up unnecessary roadblocks.

To help alleviate the "us versus them" divide and to streamline the process, the manager instituted a new policy, one that was revolutionary but that worked. He told all accounts payable staff that they had the option to take one expense-paid trip a month to any job site around the country. Once these staff members began visiting the job sites and spending the day with the superintendents, they were able to get a feel for what the superintendents' jobs were like. They saw firsthand how taxing and unglamorous the fancy lunches with city planners and inspectors were. They also saw how hectic and pressure filled the field jobs were and how much skill the superintendents had. Once back in their cubicles, the accounts payable staff showed increased empathy and improved relationships with field staff that dramatically changed the situation and broke through the impasse. They began helping field staff fill out the expense forms, calling for missing information instead of rejecting the forms and generally expediting the process. A little bit of empathy went a long way in de-escalating the conflict and increasing effectiveness.

3. Call on your compassion.

Empathy requires more than just seeing things from another point of view. It requires that you extend genuine caring for the person facing a difficulty. This means showing compassion. It helps if you can remember times when you were in a similar situation or had similar feelings. For example, when was the last time you were that anxious? When have you found yourself being so defensive? How did it feel when you found yourself confused, unsure of your ability, and in over your head? Calling up your own times of distress may help you to show compassion for the feelings and situation of the other person.

The Los Angeles Police Department found a unique and effective way to develop this ability in its officers. Because of the growing Spanish-speaking population in the city, the department implemented a pilot program to send officers to live in Mexico for six weeks to learn Spanish. When the officers returned, they reported that improving their Spanish language skills was only part of what they gained. The more powerful learning for them was the compassion they now felt for immigrants. They said they would never look at another newcomer in the same way because they had a deeper understanding of what it felt like to be the outsider in a culture, not knowing the language and finding the norms and rules baffling.

4. Communicate your understanding both verbally and nonverbally.

Empathy requires that you not only understand but that you let others know you understand what they might be feeling. This does not mean you agree or approve. Rather, it shows that you realize that they have a right to feel that way. You can express this understanding by saying, for example, "This is really frustrating" or "I can imagine how upsetting this must be." However, your nonverbal messages may be even more powerful. The concern on your face, the openness in your attitude, the full attention you give the person, and the tone of your voice also speak volumes. One telephone company supervisor demonstrated this powerfully. He found that all the empathy statements in the world were not as helpful as his behavior when he saw that one of his linemen was in distress. He would just say, "Let's go talk," and he would sit down with the employee who was facing a tough situation and just listen. His behavior said, "I see you are facing some problems. I care, and I want to help."

Practicing Empathy

The four steps to developing empathy are easier to read about than to actually do. Practice this process by choosing someone with whom you are having a difficult time and then apply these steps to that relationship. See if taking the following four actions helps you change your approach to the individual and improve your interactions and ability to be effective in working with him or her.

1. Suspend judgment about a person whose behavior is difficult for you, and replace the judgment with curiosity.

2. Abandon your perspective, and find a way to see it from the other person's experience and point of view.

3. Call on your compassion by remembering times when you might have been in a similar situation or had similar feelings.

4. Communicate your understanding by letting the person know you care and can relate.

Responding with Empathy to Unblock Communication

One of the most helpful times to use empathy is in responding to the feelings of others, especially when someone is upset. Empathy has the power to warm relations between people when there is tension, calm others when their feathers get ruffled, and soothe them when anger and fear take over. In emotionally charged situations, feelings come first, and when you respond to the emotions, you help calm the individual and enable him or her to hear you and deal with the issue at hand effectively. If you do not deal with the feelings, you won't be able to be effective, and neither will the other person. Responding with empathy does not solve the problem or fix the situation, but it enables the feelings to be dealt with so they dissipate like a fog lifting. Then the issue can be addressed more effectively.

Let's be clear first about what responding with empathy is and is not. Empathy is acknowledging and accepting someone's feelings, relating to the feelings if you can, and showing the person you understand. It does not mean you agree with the person, and it is not problem solving, giving the facts, or being reassuring. It is saying, "It must be really frustrating to have to scrap this project after all the work you've done on it." It is not saying, "Well, you knew there was a chance it would be scrapped" or "I'm sure there will be another chance to complete it when money comes in next quarter" or "That's the breaks. Money comes and money goes." It is letting the person know you understand by saying, "It is really frustrating not to be able to understand or be understood because of language differences." It is not saying, "Well you know you can give them the instructions translated into their language." While this second statement might be helpful later, it probably won't be heard or seen as helpful until the feelings of irritation are acknowledged and dealt with.

Practice creating some empathetic responses to a situation you have dealt with where the emotions of the other person blocked communication. For example, perhaps one of your colleagues says, "I'm so sick of hearing about diversity. What about us white guys? Don't we count?" First, identify the feelings. This individual sounds irritated with the changes and perhaps fearful about losing the comfort of the way things have always been. Or he may be angry because he feels he is losing his place in the order of things. Once you identify the feelings, find ways to accept and acknowledge them and relate to them if you can. You might say, "Yeah, I hear you. It's tough to deal with these changes. Sometimes you wonder where you fit," or you might say, "It doesn't feel good to be overlooked."

Try to create your own empathetic response now:

Statement of the other individual _____

Identify the feelings _____

Acknowledge the feelings and relate if you can _____

_____

Empathy works only when it is sincere, so you cannot show it effectively if you do not feel it. That's why it is often most difficult to demonstrate empathy when you are irritated, frustrated, or upset with the other person. In situations where you are emotionally blocked and find it hard to be empathetic, one technique that can help clear away feelings that are blocking you is to let yourself vent your irritation silently to yourself first. Let yourself think of the least empathetic, most sarcastic comment you could make. "Here's a quarter.

Call someone who cares" or "Get over it!" or "Grow up!" might come to mind. Once you have given your emotions a silent outlet, you may find it easier to dig deeper and reach out to the other person.

Maps to Help You Use Intercultural Literacy

Now that you have learned about Intercultural Literacy, create a plan to apply this knowledge and increase your competence in reading others accurately so you can work with them more effectively.

Map 1. Make a point to learn about the cultural whys behind behavior. Identify two or three cultures with which you work, and make a plan to learn more about the orientation, norms, and preferences of each. Don't restrict your thinking to race, gender, and ethnicity only. Perhaps you deal with different generational groups and you would like to learn more about Generation Xers or baby boomers. Maybe it would help if you learned more about employees who have some physical challenges, such as those who are deaf, vision impaired, or in wheelchairs. Perhaps you are dealing with religious differences and would like to learn more about the beliefs and practices of Muslims, Buddhists, or Mormons. Once you've decided on your groups, come up with a plan for learning about them. Identify resources, individuals, and groups that can help you learn. Maybe there is a refugee resettlement agency where you can volunteer, an organization that provides education about a particular group, or an employee association in your own company that can help you.

Map 2. Look for the upsides and downsides of all cultural norms. Think of some of the behaviors and practices you continue to have a difficult time with at work, especially those that trigger an emotional response in you. Once you have identified them, challenge yourself to see some positives in them or find ways that they benefit the team or organization.

Map 3. Continue to challenge yourself to transcend your own perspective and show empathy. Find a way to practice walking in the shoes of others. You can volunteer at a food bank, homeless shelter, or other community center. Or maybe you can plan to spend time in another culture on an extended visit or sabbatical. Or make it a habit to have lunch with a different staff member each week, getting to understand his or her life and challenges. In whatever environment you choose, focus on getting a different perspective.

The Next Steps

The essence of Intercultural Literacy is understanding that your own cultural software is not universal and that the more you learn about the cultures, rules, values, and preferences of others, the better you will be able to work with them. Edward T. Hall, one of the fathers of the field of intercultural communication, tells us, "We are all captives of culture." Intercultural Literacy is a critical tool for loosening the bonds of your captivity. The next chapter will give you the opportunity to use these skills in creating an inviting and inclusive work environment.

6

Social Architecting— Enrolling and Engaging Others

Social Architecting is about being an engineer or an architect who designs spaces intentionally to produce a climate of energy and productivity. How many of the words on the following list characterize your current work environment? Think of the best place you have ever worked. How many of these qualities describe that work environment? Whatever your answer, the feelings triggered by these qualities are the heart and soul of an effective work climate. The more of these feelings you can engineer in your work environment, the more engaged and productive your workforce will be.

- Stimulating
- Energizing
- Compelling
- Fun
- Enticing
- Engaging
- Inspiring
- Meaningful
- Productive

- Emotionally safe

- Encouraging

- Rejuvenating

- Purposeful

- Trusting

We have never met the manager who doesn't want excellent results and a good climate. But high-performing work climates don't happen by accident. They are intentionally crafted by a leader or manager who not only understands human behavior but knows what invigorates and stimulates people to give their all. Work environments can be consciously, purposefully guided and structured to yield the essence of the qualities on the above list. As a manager, you are the one who fashions the type of workplace you will have. You just have to decide what kind of workplace you want yours to be, and then you design and structure it.

Social Architecting is appropriately the last component of the EID Model because it uses the learnings from the prior three components and applies them in a way that works for the good of the individuals and the team. The underlying premise of Social Architecting is that each individual can and must make a positive difference in the work environment. No person or action is irrelevant, and no manager or team leader has the sole responsibility for creating the atmosphere. The little kindnesses one does, the attempt to really understand different points of view in a respectful way, the acknowledgment of different talents and strengths as adding value, the unintrusive but appropriate interest shown about parts of people's lives beyond work—all of these matter. Every person in a work group can demonstrate caring, support, accountability, flexibility, and understanding. Every person can strive to give unthreatening but clear feedback and help be a problem solver. As a manager, you not only model but can also help employees be committed and hold everyone accountable for making a positive difference in the workplace and for *intentionally* choosing to behave in ways that are constructive, purposeful, productive, and healthy. Social Architecting helps you produce results with clients, end users, stockholders, and co-workers.

Effective Social Architecting shows up in how employees feel about where they work. Clues always exist. Start noticing; become a Sherlock Holmes in your workplace. For starters, look for ownership of the workplace. Do employees feel like the place is theirs? Two stories, one at a manufacturing plant and one at a school, make that point. The message in both cases is this: When you don't feel connected to a place, you don't care about it, and you don't treat it like it is yours. Performance will reflect the caring or lack of caring and connection, sometimes through some unusual measures of performance.

The Manufacturing Plant

In a manufacturing plant, we asked those in charge what their criteria would be for a successful diversity change initiative. Their measure was "the restrooms." We were a bit surprised and wanted to make sure we understood correctly. "The restrooms?" we asked. We heard it right. They told us that when the urinals were no longer kicked off the walls, when graffiti was no longer all over the place, when paper was thrown in the trash cans instead of on the floor, they would know that they had a place people owned and felt a part of. In short, employees would treat the place as though it was theirs. An unusual clue to be sure, but meaningful and relevant.

The School

A large urban school district had invested large amounts of money on building beautiful new state-of-the-art schools. We saw pictures of them when they opened—magnificent! We saw them two years later, and the difference between the original school and the school two years later was both dramatic and tragic. The lack of ownership by the students and the lack of commitment to keeping the school pristine demonstrated a number of things, one of them the lack of positive Social Architecting and hence the lack of ownership felt by the students and the school community.

These are dramatic examples of what happens in the absence of clear expectations in the form of unambiguous statements about directly influencing and shaping an environment. Think about both the emotional and practical consequences to people and buildings when there is a lack of investment or energy in a workplace, and also think about how your workplace compares to these two examples. The following questions are a starting point for being introspective enough to shed light on your organization and may indicate a need to enhance your social architecting.

- **Different perspectives:** How able are people to grasp different perspectives and realities and to build bridges across these differences? How might the inability to bridge differences have an impact on openness, flexibility, and collaboration?

- **Team members:** Reflect on the members who are part of the team. Who do people shy away from for being negative, mean, or unwilling to be a team player? If the answer is "No one," great. If names of people surface, you have opportunities for coaching.

- **Norms:** What norms permeate the group? Are there norms such as cliques or lateness that no one talks about but that most people have negative feelings about? What might the absence of dialogue, on this or other issues, indicate about trust in your group?

- **Communication processes:** When people have different values, priorities, or perspectives, what communication and feedback processes will get you through these conflicts? As a manager, how do you model dealing with these kinds of differences?

- **Engagement:** How do team members demonstrate real engagement in and commitment to the tasks, to other team members, and to the organization? You can get a partial answer to this question by looking at how team members exceed your expectations and their own in order to get the work done.

The answers to these questions offer a quick snapshot of how developed your Social Architecting skills and those of your team are. Although you may have many good things happening under the Social Architecting umbrella, your team and organization can do better. This chapter will show you how.

There are four components of Social Architecting.

Components of Social Architecting

▪ Serving as a cultural interpreter

▪ Communicating effectively

▪ Resolving conflicts in diverse settings

▪ Structuring a synergistic and compelling environment

Each of these four parts gives you necessary tools and skills to build a rich and inviting environment where employees want to give their best.

Serving as a Cultural Interpreter

Inside yourself or outside, you never have to change what you see, only the way you see it.

—THADDEUS GOLAS

In today's complex, globalized world, there is always a need to bridge differences and build understanding. After experiencing so many cultural dilemmas and misinterpretations in our client organizations, we used to say, "You need to hire a cultural interpreter." Over time, with enough repeated misunderstandings, we had an epiphany. Organizations don't need to hire this expertise in one particular person. They need to develop this skill among their employees. While some people will be better at it than others, it is an essential competence for all employees.

Being a cultural interpreter means that you are multilingual in behaviors. You can translate or decode behavior. You don't expect or desire people to be like you. Using Intercultural Literacy knowledge, cultural interpreters help others understand possible meanings of behavior as opposed to misinterpreting it. Cultural interpreters consider numerous explanations for someone's actions. For example, if someone won't shake your hand when you meet in the business world, you would consider, and help others see, the possibility that religious observances preclude doing that across gender lines. A devout Muslim or an Orthodox Jew, for example, may not shake the hand of a person of the opposite gender because of a religious practice, not an act of discounting or demeaning someone. If a person comes in for a job interview and has a difficult time extolling his own virtues and successes, you consider that he may be from a collectivist culture where one does not proclaim virtue in one's own behavior or take credit for success without attributing performance to the whole group. A cultural interpreter helps fellow employees learn to resist the perception that, in this case, someone is timid or lacking confidence.

Steps to Serving as a Cultural Interpreter

Serving as a cultural interpreter involves a series of useful steps that can change an outcome, the dynamics of a relationship, or the entire climate in a work group. Developing this skill is a concrete and doable four-step process.

1. Be aware of your first reaction to and interpretation of an event.

Understanding your first reactions, or helping others understand theirs, is essential. How you interpret an event influences how you react. In the best-case scenario, harmony and understanding result. In the worst-case scenario, frustration, disrespect, and discounting of someone result. One of the things we hear about in many organizations when they try to recruit and hire people of different backgrounds is that a soft handshake ruins a candidate's chances. We are told repeatedly that not giving a firm handshake in an interview can cause a hiring panel to totally discount and write off a candidate. When a cultural interpreter helps hiring panel members learn about a broader array of cultural norms—a soft handshake in some cultures is a sign of warmth and connection or a concession to the Western business practice of handshakes—the hiring panel members become more open to the candidate. The entire ritual and tone of meeting and connecting with a potential new hire can change with that one interpretation.

2. Step into a judgment-free zone.

The second step to becoming a cultural interpreter is to intentionally remain neutral at first. Not assigning any judgment to a person's behavior is critical. In the last example, when someone gives a soft handshake in an interview to members of a hiring panel, usually a member of the panel comments about this candidate having too little confidence and not being assertive enough. This is a moment when the cultural interpreter can teach, by not only sharing information and knowledge but also challenging the interpretation of the soft handshake. The cultural interpreter has the opportunity to coach hiring panel members to avoid making any judgments at all for the moment and can help them reinterpret that behavior and file all of their reactions in a judgment-free zone till a later time when the candidate can be assessed for multiple skill factors.

3. Identify alternative ways of understanding.

Asking the question "What else could this mean?" provides insight and understanding. In the case of the hiring committee, a cultural interpreter can ask the group for alternative reasons, besides lack of confidence, that a person might offer a soft handshake. The following list of possible reasons might emerge from your question. A soft handshake could be the result of

- A cultural norm or preference for a soft handshake
- Arthritis, which makes sturdy handshakes too painful
- A feeling that a handshake is a concession to Western norms, along with a preference for another greeting such as bowing or kissing on both cheeks
- A reluctance to shake hands at all across gender due to religious beliefs.

Considering many possible interpretations is one way of introducing some of the prevailing norms of other cultural groups and preferences of individuals. The new knowledge usually results in people having greater openness and making fewer initial assumptions about how to interpret a behavior.

4. Have a repertoire of responses to the situation.

As discussed earlier, humans have a need for control and approval. Giving people more options leads to feelings of increased control, feeling powerful rather than boxed in. The more you can help people be flexible in their thinking or interpretation of events, the greater the chance of seeing that flexibility reflected in their own behavior. Flexibility comes from a lack of fear and leads to a more generous, open spirit. The last step in being a cultural interpreter is to use your broadened understanding of behaviors to find more effective ways to respond.

A cultural interpreter can work one-on-one or with a few people at a time. On occasion a cultural interpreter can also work with a large group. We observed one such situation in a health care setting, where language differences often spark deep conflict because patients and their families get justifiably anxious when they can't understand or communicate with their caregivers. In this story, the conflict was between two groups of nurses.

The Nurses

In a large hospital one group of nurses was born and reared in the United States, with English as their native language. The second group of nurses had been recruited from the Philippines, and while they did speak English with varying degrees of fluency or competence, Tagalog was their native tongue. The hospital policy was to speak English to patients and families, and when on the floor, speaking English was expected at all times. A conflict erupted in an auditorium full of nurses because the Filipino nurses often reverted to their native language when not working with patients.

One nurse manager from the Philippines changed the whole tone, understanding, and definition of the situation. As the conflict escalated into shouting, she told the group she wanted to say something. She knew her own feeling about the demands of speaking all day in a second language. She could also see how the U.S.-born nurses felt excluded and intentionally left out, annoyed at policy not being adhered to, and worst of all, talked about by others. She also knew that the Filipino nurses felt demeaned and devalued because in casual situations they were looked down on for speaking their native language, and they felt that they had the right to speak their first language. They also felt that they could communicate more accurately and quickly in Tagalog.

Showing her skill as a cultural interpreter, the nurse manager spoke to the group. She said that the policy of the hospital is to speak English in front of patients and families. She knew that, she expected that of her Filipino staff, and that was nonnegotiable. Then she told the group something else. This manager, who was totally fluent in English, told the group how stressful and demanding it is to think in a second language all day, especially in their high-stress environment. She explained to the group that although she is fluent in English, speaking English can never compare to the comfort she feels when slipping back into her native tongue. She talked about the stress of the job and the comfort of being able to have lunch with people who speak Tagalog.

The nurse manager combined the steps of serving as a cultural interpreter with those of being empathetic. Everyone in that room who was monolingual reinterpreted the Filipino nurses' behavior because they had visions of working in China, Russia, Mexico, or the Philippines, and in that instant they got it. Even being fluent in two or more languages would not be a substitute for comfort in English, their first language. This example diffused the emotional tone of the discussion and provided an opportunity to create options that would work for everyone around language use at work.

> *I could save myself a lot of wear and tear with people if I just*
> *learned to understand them.*
> —RALPH ELLISON

Maps to Help You Become a Cultural Interpreter

The following suggestions will help you develop competence in this area and bring greater understanding and connection to people on your team or in one-on-one relationships.

Map 1: Activate your radar. Pay attention to and be in tune with the nuances of cultural differences, and provide opportunities to help spread understanding. We don't mean to suggest that you do it in a know-it-all kind of way. But acknowledging the rubs between people with some nonjudgmental statements such as "Have you considered . . . " or "Think about this from a different cultural vantage point" or "What else might it mean or imply?" can be helpful. Your first step is to be mindful of the importance and consequences of culture.

Map 2: Stop . . . look . . . listen. Once you have activated the radar in the first step, follow up by paying attention, observing, and really listening to people. Then be knowledgeable and open enough to at least consider what misinterpretations or irritations might be at play. By noticing and focusing on the assumptions but not judging them, you can find ways to give people feedback about norms, reactions, and behaviors so deeply embedded that they may be unaware of them.

Map 3: Have an open heart and mind. Your ability to be an even, honest broker with no hidden agendas and no advocacy for any particular person or group is essential to being an effective cultural interpreter. This means that as a manager and a human being, you have the equivalent of 360-degree vision. You see things in their totality and then help translate what you see to others, thus enabling them to get a bigger, broader perspective.

Map 4: Develop the skill of asking good questions in ways that are non-judgmental and don't produce defensiveness. As a cultural interpreter, you are part information dispenser because there are, in fact, very different and specific cultural norms that do affect how people respond to events and interpret the behavior of others. For you to help someone understand that downcast eyes can be a sign of respect rather than deceit can be critical. But beyond that concrete knowledge, you have the chance to ask employees important questions such as the following:

- If you ask a job applicant to discuss his strengths and accomplishments in his last job and he can't do it without talking about the whole team, does it matter to you? If so, why? What is your thinking?

- What difference might the applicant's answer make to you if you understand that he is from a collectivist culture where the team is the focus rather than the individual?

- Since there is no individualistic socket for this potential employee to plug into, what would make it possible for you to consider him?

By asking these kinds of questions, you are offering necessary information that can help both parties bridge differences.

Map 5: Keep practicing your skills, and maintain a log or journal of the outcomes. When things work out well, make notes about why. What did you do, what did you say, or how did you approach this interaction that worked? Keeping a log will enable you to see your patterns and give you perspective on which patterns are worth repeating. You will also have experiences that result in less satisfying conclusions. Maintain a log about those as well, with a particular emphasis on what you would do differently next time.

You can practice your skills at work, at home, in the community, and everywhere you go, and as you know, practice makes perfect.

Communicating Effectively

Am I not destroying my enemies when I
make them friends of mine?
—ABRAHAM LINCOLN

Effective communication and conflict resolution are central to the quality of every relationship you have in life. This section addresses communication effectiveness in your role as a manager, trainer, coach, or human resources or organization development professional, but the skills and tools translate to any area of your life.

Flexible Communication

Effective communication starts with acknowledgment of the fact that you cannot develop a single style that works equally well with everyone. Adaptation is key, whether you are talking about varying your style because of an individual's age, education level, socioeconomics, geography, language, or thinking and problem-solving style. All of these differences, and many more, affect your ability to communicate well with others, develop relationships, bridge differences, create understanding, and solve problems. Most human beings have habits or preferred styles of communicating in the face of differences. This component of Social Architecting helps you understand your habits, preferences, and skills. Then it suggests that you develop others as well so you will be even more effective across a wide range of differences.

Think about different communication styles you have experienced and their impact on you. Some people are direct and to the point. Many people relish this conciseness, finding that brevity welcome, but that communication style may be a little sparse and succinct for others. Other people give copious details when they communicate, going into every ramification as they share information and tell their story. For some the detail is enriching; for others, it is maddening. There are many styles between these two extremes. No particular style is better or worse. They all have benefits and downsides. Which of these styles is closer to your way of communicating? To be effective in a diverse environment you need to develop adaptability, patience, and ultimately tools for communicating well and resolving the inevitable conflicts that happen, even in the best of relationships. As a manager, you need to help others develop these abilities as well.

The advantages of being able to shift styles and adapt to various audiences are huge. Two memorable examples, one that worked and one that didn't, provide lessons in communication.

The Head of Diversity

We met with a man who was the head of diversity for a large entertainment studio. The man had gotten support for diversity in an industry that generally focuses only on weekend grosses at the box office or TV ratings. We asked this African American how he was able to get support from the white executive team. He told us that "doing lunch" is a big thing in Hollywood, and so is relationship building.

Effective communication for this studio executive meant taking someone to lunch every single day. He found that this was the way to create relationship, awareness, support, and understanding. He did a lot of listening. He paid attention to the style of the person he was with and focused on giving time, respect, and appropriate communication to each individual. One person at a time, he courted their backing so they would become advocates and supporters—or at least not saboteurs. It was an exhausting, labor-intensive, intentional process. He would have liked to find an easier, quicker, and more direct method, but in the end he got the support he needed. This personal attention and investment of time in getting to know the power brokers at the studio and what style worked for each paid big dividends.

The Vice President of Human Resources

A children's hospital in a large urban area had a diverse population, with people coming from all over the world to have their children treated and cared for. The steady demographic changes meant that one-size-fits-all management would no longer work, but the hospital had no management development program.

A woman stepped in who was good at learning the particular gaps of the managers who needed training. She designed for these managers on-target programs to fill their knowledge gaps. Her communication style was based on building relationships. There were 2,700 people in this organization, and she knew them all. Her preferred way of doing needs assessments was to talk to employees, one at a time in interviews or in the cafeteria for a cup of coffee, to really hear their realities so she could offer them classes with the precise skills and knowledge they needed.

We were following this woman's progress, but one day we found out she had been fired. We were aghast: she had crafted a well-attended and on-target management development program. Her boss told us his reason for her dismissal: "She was always walking around and talking to people and was never in her office."

These two people had very different communication styles. One was interactive and person to person: nothing about it was formal or structured. Her boss's style was the opposite. He did not see the great results she was getting. Rather, he saw an annoying style of socializing and what looked like kibitzing when he thought she should have been at her desk.

Style shifting requires you to think about the person you need to interact with and how he or she likes to be talked to. Does the person prefer conversation to be concise, direct, and to the point? Or does he or she prefer ten to fifteen minutes of small talk so relationships can be established before any real transaction takes place? Whatever the preferences are, they matter.

Identify people you interact with most, and pay attention to what styles they have. Which of their patterns match yours? Might you be more effective if you style shifted with some of them a little? Think about it and look for opportunities to make it happen.

"Know thyself," the dictum of Socrates, is a critical thread throughout this book. Employees have individual and collective responsibility for influencing the environment, one person at a time. When you style shift, you can influence your environment in a positive way. Communication is always going on, but what is the quality of it? Does this communication produce the result you are looking for? Creating a healthy work climate depends on people having a clear sense of their impact on others and then shifting accordingly. Someone once said that the listener controls the conversation. We would adapt this to say that the person who is an observer and style shifter controls not only the conversation but also the results.

To see how flexible and adaptable you are, rate the behaviors in Activity 14 that require style shifting on your part.

Activity 14

Shifting Communication Styles

Mark each style as an easy or difficult one for you to shift to:

E—Easy for me to deal with; I can style shift.

D—Difficult for me to deal with; don't know if I can stretch enough.

_____ 1. Communications are direct and to the point.

_____ 2. Communications are detailed and specific.

_____ 3. Communications are indirect and circular.

_____ 4. Communications are general and open ended.

_____ 5. Communications frame issues positively.

_____ 6. Communications take a critical slant.

_____ 7. Communications are objective and take a balanced view with little emotion.

_____ 8. Communications are open and self-disclosing.

_____ 9. Communications are formal and private.

_____10. Communications deal only with factual content.

The biggest mistake is believing there is one right way to listen, to talk, to have a conversation, or a relationship.

—DEBORAH TANNEN,
You Just Don't Understand

This is a good time to use the mirror to develop your ability to communicate effectively. Check your reflection and use the following questions to see more vividly how you affect others.

1. Observe people's behavior toward you, not just in their greetings but in their nonverbal cues. See how relaxed they appear, or how anxious and maybe even intimidated they seem to be. Make a mental note of the cues that give you the information. What are you basing your observations on? What cues do you wish you were seeing?

2. Check out your perceptions. Compare people's reaction to you with their interactions and reactions to others. Some differences you observe may be due to formal title in the organization, but not all of it. What do you notice? How are their tone, language, and body language different with you than with others?

3. If you observe noticeable differences in relationships and interactions that you don't like, seek feedback, both directly and indirectly. Have a conversation, perhaps informally, with the person. Inquire specifically about any ways you might help the employee be more effective and feel more engaged. If particular issues in the workplace are of concern, balance between asking general questions, such as "How are things going?" and specific questions, such as "What's working well in your relationships and communication with others? What do you wish you did better?" You can close the conversation by asking, "What do you need more or less of from me?"

Resolving Conflicts in Diverse Settings

The inclusive, safe, and open environment you are trying to create sets off alarm bells when differences aren't resolved to the satisfaction of everyone involved. At the very least, you want and need to solicit, use, and leverage different points of view. In the best of all worlds, you model how to give and receive feedback in helpful, nonthreatening ways that minimize conflict and maximize synergy.

Shifting your communication style so that it is more responsive to each person is helpful in maximizing the effectiveness of your communications. But even being a great adapter or style shifter will not avoid conflict altogether. There are times when you will have differences with others that seem intractable. Sometimes the real issues are not discussed. It might be difficult for you to say to an employee, "When you challenged me in that meeting, I felt discounted and demeaned. I felt as though I lost face with the group." That not only might be a difficult sentiment to articulate or conceptualize in your own head but would take both trust and courage to talk about with someone else. It might feel risky and vulnerable. However, being honest and insightful enough to describe the feelings, first to yourself and then eventually to the other person, makes a big difference in the quality, longevity, and effectiveness of your relationships.

Steps to Getting to the Heart of the Matter

We have developed a four-step process that enables you to get to the essence of the difficulty in situations where feelings can cause defensiveness and cloud the issue. You can then communicate clearly and fully to resolve the situation. We call the method Heart-of-the-Matter Conversations. The four steps are:

1. **Sensory conversation**—see reality and describe it.

2. **Brain conversation**—talk about assumptions you might make as you interpret the other person's behavior.

3. **Feeling conversation**—label your feelings.

4. **Soul conversation**—articulate what you'd like or expect as an outcome.

Figure 5 illustrates each step using an example we see frequently in the workplace: the appropriate start time for meetings. In this case, the start time was determined as a result of a lengthy group discussion by all team members. Everyone bought in, but one team member continued to come late.

As you can see, the thrust behind this four-stage process is not punitive or finger pointing. It makes use of "I messages" and avoids the blaming use of

---

Figure 5

Four Steps for Heart-of-the-Matter Conversations

1. Sensory Conversation—facts

Describe the situation or behavior:

"The meeting started at 9:00 as everyone agreed to. You continue to come in at 9:20."

"This is the third meeting at which you've arrived at 9:20."

2. Brain conversation—assumptions

Describe your interpretation of the situation or behavior:

"After a group discussion and an agreement to start at 9:00, you seem not to care about the decision we made together because you are still coming when you want to."

"You must be having some problems that prevent you from getting here on time."

"Since you are not here at our agreed-upon meeting time, you seem to make other things a higher priority."

3. Feeling conversation—emotions

Describe feelings and reactions you have:

"I am disappointed. I thought we had an understanding and an agreement."

"After our conversation and agreement, I feel betrayed."

"Frankly, I am annoyed."

4. Soul conversation—hopes and expectations

Explain what you want, need, and expect:

"I need you to keep your commitment and show up on time."

"I need some suggestions from you about how to resolve this issue."

"I need your input about a way to honor the group's commitment to meeting times in a way that works for everyone and has all of us make good on our responsibilities."

"you." It requires you to own your feelings and to express them in a nonthreatening way. This method draws on the introspective process from Affirmative Introspection and on numerous processes from Self-Governance for dealing with change, ambiguity, and emotions. It also calls for empathy in trying to understand another person's reality. But finally it is about being the architect of your own interactions and relationships. This four-step Heart-of-the-Matter Conversations tool fosters your ability to articulate your feelings after you have taken the step to see reality as it is. No rose-colored glasses are allowed here. This is a portable, useful tool that will enable you to be a superb communicator, in conflict or not, by being clear, open, and honest and by dealing with emotions in a calm, nonthreatening way.

Maps to Help You Use Heart-of-the-Matter Conversations

There are a number of ways you can enhance your use of Heart-of-the-Matter Conversations. Following are some suggestions.

Map 1: Keep a journal reserved especially for difficult situations. Write these four steps down every time. Look for patterns, and determine how you will either interpret situations differently or act in ways that are new and courageous for you. The patterns are critical because you may be getting hooked over and over again by what you interpret as a lack of respect, as being discounted, or as people not owning up to their commitments. Patterns count—yours and those of others—but you can change only your own perceptions and reactions when you are aware of them.

Map 2: Focus on each part of the process when you have a conflict. Notice which parts are difficult, but also notice in which parts you are having more ease and effectiveness. Where you are having difficulty, dig deep. Get to the bottom of the problem to understand why, and then reinterpret any harmful messages you are telling yourself. The way you are interpreting a behavior may significantly influence your intensity, flexibility, and openness. For example, if you are expecting a phone call that does not come, your feelings about it will vary depending on the following interpretations:

- "I know how busy he is, and he'll call when he can."

- "He is so trustworthy that I am worried about him. It is not like him to miss even a phone call."

- "He doesn't care about me. I don't matter. If this were someone else, he'd have called already."

Map 3: As you start to get upset, focus on the question "What else could this mean?" Brainstorm multiple interpretations. Notice changes in the intensity of your feelings when you come up with other possible meanings. How do you explain the changes in your attitude and the intensity of your feelings?

The more you use the Heart-of-the-Matter Conversations tool, the more proficient you will become, and the more a part of you it will become. There is no time like the present to begin.

Structuring a Synergistic and Compelling Environment

No culture can live if it attempts to be exclusive.

—MAHATMA GANDHI

The third component of Social Architecting focuses on the environment you help create. In this part you identify the elements that you want to consciously and intentionally create in order to build that safe space that is compelling and captivating and that makes people want to show up to work for more than a paycheck. Much of the makeup of a compelling environment is intangible. Years ago, we did research for a class in effective problem solving and decision making. After reading twenty different books, all long and complex, we realized a profound and simple truth. If you want people to show up to the workplace with energy and engagement, with purpose, passion and productivity, both their ego needs and affiliation needs must be met. Think about the interpersonal dynamics in your work group. At the end of a day of working together, do people usually feel valued for their contributions? Do they feel their presence has made a difference? Do they feel they accomplished anything? Do they feel they made anyone's life better? Have they laughed, had fun together, and felt as though they had an important place at the table? Do they think their participation matters? How you answer these questions while you think about your group will go a long way toward telling you how compelling and synergistic you perceive your environment to be. More important, however, is

---

Activity 15

How Engaging Is Your Work Environment?

Read each of the high-engagement factors in the list below. If the factor is true of your work group, check the Yes box; if not, check the No box.

High-Engagement Factors	Yes	No
I feel as if my presence makes a positive difference.		
Our environment is inclusive.		
When someone is absent, we notice and care.		
Ours is a group of significant accomplishment.		
We appreciate individual differences and the contribution each person brings to the group.		
We have fun together as we do our work.		
We have a sense of connection between team members.		
We always come through on our tasks.		
We strive to understand the different backgrounds of our team members and the richness these differences bring.		
In this work group, I can be who I genuinely am and feel valued for it.		

---

what your employees would say. Use Activity 15 to help assess how engaging your work environment is.

Not only people's ego needs but their affiliation needs must be met. In your group, how connected do people feel to one another? Do they have a sense of belonging and being part of the group? When members of the group are gone, does anyone notice or care? And when people return, are they welcomed and acknowledged? Can people express their uniqueness? These criteria may seem obvious and insignificant, but actually managing people in a way in which their presence or absence is noticed and in which differences inspire and delight rather than irritate and annoy is no small thing. This kind of environment can be created by allowing people to be known for who they are—complete with their many beliefs, talents, strengths, and vulnerabilities. An appreciation of the complexity of all team members and an honoring of these differences while also proclaiming some important common ground is a necessary beginning.

The story "The Insurance Company" is about an experience we had with an organization years ago. The group in the anecdote showed that work doesn't have to be grim business and that environments don't have to be toxic and unhealthy.

The Insurance Company

The insurance company had four diversity councils that met once a month, and each was charged with a different task.

The organizational commitment was huge because every month employees were brought to a central location from all over the western United States. The councils had one year to create systems, policies, and procedures that would change the organization. At the six-month mark, they had to present findings and recommendations to the company's top one hundred executives for feedback. This story is about the night before the presentation to the top executives.

Council members arrived about four o'clock in the afternoon and got to work immediately. The teams wanted to be flawless and ready for anything in their presentations. As facilitators/observers, we noticed how much fun and purpose one group found in working together. They teased, joked, and laughed, but never at the expense of getting the work done. The different talents and skills of the members were put to use. The person who was the computer whiz took care of the Power-Point presentation. Others were good writers, designers of the material, and administrators who oversaw the whole process, and everyone had a unique niche that was necessary without being redundant.

Between five and six o'clock as employees were leaving at the end of their workday, they stuck their head in the room to see what all the noise was about. They jokingly admonished and reprimanded the members of this council for laughing too loudly, having too much fun, and not being serious enough. But the eyes of these exiting employees spoke volumes of longing and an unstated question: "How come I don't have that kind of camaraderie and fun at work? I want it."

The council stayed and worked diligently until 8:30 that night and cut no corners in their task, but the high level of trust and the appreciation of unique interests, talents, and skills made what could have been a very long workday seem purposeful, productive, meaningful, and fun.

Defining a Compelling Environment: A Good Place to Start

You become a social architect when you intentionally shape the environment in positive ways, by design. Start by describing the top six or eight descriptors—behaviors, values, or conditions—that you would like to have characterize your work environment. When we three authors do this periodically for our own EID partnership, a few differences come up, but words such as *integrity, trust, making a difference, accountability, appreciation of our uniqueness, creativity,* and *having fun and laughter as a shared experience* always appear. When you do this exercise, make sure you limit the number of choices so that you can see what your top priorities are. Forced choices always heighten the clarification of your top values. With limited resources of time, energy, and money, you can't have everything, so what matters most to you? Do this for yourself; then ask for feedback and input from the people who report to you. One CEO talked about the importance of diversity, but every time a decision had to be made about resource allocation, diversity moved farther down the list of priorities. You know what you say matters most to you in creating a compelling environment, but the feedback from others will tell you if you are really true to your words or are just giving lip service to them.

To create a compelling environment that leads to high performance and engagement, use the following four-step process with your team or work group:

1. Write priorities individually.

Ask each person to identify his or her top six to eight descriptors of a compelling work environment and write them on a round piece of paper divided into slices like a pie or on a triangular piece of paper divided into a pyramid structure. The pie conveys the idea that all values and behaviors are equally important while the pyramid conveys a hierarchical structure. The top level of a pyramid can indicate greater importance, or the bottom level can be more important because it is more foundational; the meaning you assign to the pyramid structure is up to you.

2. Share and discuss priorities.

Once each person writes his or her top six to eight descriptors of a compelling environment, have people share them and collectively discuss and reach an agreement on them. Chart the agreed-upon qualities. Sometimes this is a simple process where words like *integrity* and *honesty* mean almost the same thing. At other times you can lead the group through a rich discussion in which significant differences emerge. Creativity may be hugely important to one person, while continuous learning matters to someone else who feels that creativity is of lesser importance. Remember that there are no right or wrong answers. You can function as a cultural interpreter by helping people understand that they may be after the same things but are stating their ideas and desires differently. Semantics matter. You can also be a skilled facilitator or bridge builder in helping negotiate real differences. If someone is task oriented and wants to focus on outcomes and accountability, you will have an opportunity to facilitate dialogue between this person and the one who mostly cares about process and focuses on relationships and how to increase respect or engagement.

3. Identify progress.

After the group reaches consensus, give each person a package of green, yellow, and red dots. On the chart that publicly states what collective environment the group wants, have people put their dots. The three color dots will give each person a chance to indicate whether or not he or she thinks that each descriptor is already accomplished, a work in progress, or hardly even started.

- **Green dots:** We have achieved this. Fabulous. We need to maintain this, but it is already a reality.

- **Yellow dots:** Sometimes we have this in the work environment, and sometimes we don't. We are not consistent.

- **Red dots:** I have yet to see this in our work environment. It would be a strange phenomenon here.

4. Identify action steps and responsibilities.

The whole group then looks at the accumulation of green, yellow, and red dots. That quick assessment is the beginning of a conversation and the creation of action steps that lead to people assuming individual and collective responsibility for creating the desired compelling environment you all have identified.

Continuing to Build a Compelling Environment

Looking in the mirror at the following areas will increase your insight and ultimately lead to action.

- Have a vision of processes or methods you want your team or group to use in solving its differences. Once you have that mental picture, determine which of those processes you do well and are easy for you and which processes present growth opportunities.

- Under what circumstances, and with whom, do you feel comfortable giving and receiving feedback? As you assess the dynamics and relationships on your team, take note of the areas of strength. For example, people are honest and straightforward. That may be a strength, but if they are not tactful and turn others off, it could become a liability. Do your mental assessment. Think about little actions that could make a big difference.

- Determine what factors in a work environment bring a smile to your face, energy and purpose to your work, and commitment by co-workers to one another and to the organization. Then discuss how you as a group stack up in these areas. The question you continue to ask relentlessly is, Where are the growth opportunities we can work on to achieve a magnificent work environment?

Maps to Help You Build a Compelling Environment

These mirror reflections are an important part of the process. But as you know, insight and understanding are only part of the job. What actions must you take, individually and collectively? The following is a map for continuing the journey.

Map 1: Walk the talk. You have a mental picture of how you want people to solve their differences. You have opportunities to coach one-on-one, as well as the chance to teach and have conversations with the whole group. Think about who you are, or how you can model the very behaviors you seek and value. One of America's great thinkers and writers, Ralph Waldo Emerson, said, "I can't hear what you're saying because who you are rings so loudly in my ears." When it comes to listening to and observing you, if words and deeds don't match, people will take cues from your actions every time.

Map 2: Create nonthreatening ways to bring up differences. One of the most successful ways to encourage healthy, honest feedback is to have a whole-group discussion. Ask people what would help them increase trust and comfort. We have seen groups come up with key words like pinch, ouch, or boomerang as nonthreatening signals to indicate that something isn't right. Once a signal has been given, encourage people to use the Heart of the Matter Conversations process.

Map 3: Do periodic checkups. Use the compelling environment process described earlier in the chapter as either a pie chart or a pyramid. That is only step one. Once you have had the conversation about agreed-upon values and behaviors, you might want to get big blow-up charts artfully done and laminated. Post them. Also, make sure that once a month you re-visit whether or not those top six or eight descriptors are still valid, and see how the group is doing on the road to achieving them. By staying on top of this and integrating checkups into the operation of the group, you will bring energy and legitimacy to the conversation.

It is easy to perform a good action but not easy to acquire a settled habit of performing such actions.

—ARISTOTLE

There are no shortcuts to social architecting, or for that matter, to the EID process. But we highly recommend the journey. It is a path worth taking. The next two chapters will give you additional techniques for the journey.

7

Coaching Individuals for Emotional Intelligence in Your Diverse Workplace

Now that you've learned the four components of the Emotional Intelligence and Diversity Model and have practiced using the techniques for your own development, you are ready to help others on the job. No matter what your job title—manager, supervisor, trainer, HR professional, consultant, or adviser—you can become a coach for others. This chapter gives you specific ways to work with employees one-on-one as you develop, counsel, and coach them.

Affirmative Introspection—Taking a Look Inside

Employees often look outside of themselves for answers to their own failures and to explain conflicts in the workplace. By teaching introspective skills, you can help employees take responsibility for their actions—and learn from them. Introspective skills increase individuals' awareness of their impact on others, resulting in more-conscious and productive choices in the workplace.

Helping Employees Know What Makes Them Tick

When employees are experiencing strong emotional responses to situations, use the introspective process in Chapter 3 to help them get a handle on the situation. You can help employees know what makes them tick by turning the steps of the process into questions that will guide the discussion. Ask the following questions:

1. What is the event, situation, or experience that the employee is dealing with? Make sure you remind the individual to stick to the facts, the specific behaviors, and the situations and to not make judgments or assumptions.

2. What is the importance of the situation in the employee's life? Why does it matter to him or her?

3. What is the impact of the situation? What ripples and consequences does it create?

4. What feelings does the situation evoke in the employee?

5. What has the employee learned or can he or she learn from this situation?

Leading individuals through a discussion guided by the use of these questions will help them gain clarity and a sense of control over the incident, no matter how painful or difficult it is. This clarity and control will, in turn, make the situation easier to deal with effectively.

Helping Employees Be More Comfortable in Their Own Skin

To help employees discover their full potential, build their confidence, and unleash their creative potential, you need to help them build more comfort with themselves. One way to do this is to help them recognize those aspects of themselves they reject and to help them accept these aspects as part of their identity. People cannot build comfort with themselves unless first they recognize, explore, and affirm aspects of their personality and identity that they find difficult to accept.

You can help employees find comfort in themselves by asking them to do the following:

1. Identify three aspects of his or her personality and identity in which the employee feels great pride and comfort. Explore how these aspects affect him or her and others.

2. Identify three aspects of his or her personality and upbringing that the employee does not feel pride and comfort with and explore how they affect him or her and others. What is the element that brings discomfort and shame?

3. Identify one thing the employee can tell himself or herself or do to bring more acceptance and greater comfort with those rejected parts.

You can also explain to employees that becoming more comfortable with themselves takes time and is a continuous and gradual process.

Helping Employees Become Aware of Their Own Biases and Hot Buttons

To be effective in a diverse world, employees need to be aware of the norms and behaviors that trigger anger and create conflict for them. Developing an awareness of these hot buttons helps them achieve a sense of control, which prevents them from being "emotionally hijacked." You can help them become aware of their hot buttons by having them list behaviors that make them angry. Then you can discuss how they react when their buttons are pushed and how they might manage their reactions more effectively. You can even help employees explore some of the following cultural norms that frequently elicit strong reactions in the workplace:

- Attitudes about punctuality
- Practices regarding personal distance and touch
- Practices regarding the extent of self-disclosure
- Eating habits and preferences for different types of foods
- Formality or informality
- Communication styles
- Conflict-resolution styles

Using the knowledge about Intercultural Literacy that you gained in Chapter 5, discuss with your employees the possible cultural influences behind these behaviors.

Beyond having employees think about the behaviors that irritate them, you can also have them wrestle with which of their own behaviors might irritate others. Most people focus their attention on the behaviors of others that push their hot buttons but seldom think that their own norms and behaviors could function as hot buttons for others. They may be hindering their own effectiveness if they push others' buttons.

Self-Governance—Getting a Handle on Your Feelings

A key skill in dealing with others is the ability to manage emotions, especially when the impulse is to react in counterproductive ways. You can coach employees to govern their feelings by teaching appropriate ways to behave in certain situations and to maintain optimism, along with strategies for effective communication.

Helping Employees Make Ambiguity an Ally

Employees need to know how to effectively handle the ambiguity they experience when they confront a diverse world that is rapidly changing. You can help employees respond with emotional intelligence and make ambiguity an ally by doing the following:

- Coach them to take time and delay their initial impulse to react immediately (for example, taking the first option that comes to mind, terminating the contract, or avoiding the situation).

- Help employees to acknowledge their feelings rather than deny them by giving them the "Vocabulary of Emotions" list in Chapter 3 so they can identify what they are feeling in a particular situation.

- Guide employees in using the "Mental Board Members" technique presented in Chapter 4.

- Encourage employees to sit with their feelings of uncertainty and confusion when they encounter differences by helping them explore the conflicting values that arise in the dilemma and the upsides and downsides of the many options.

Helping Employees Become Change Masters

Helping employees manage change is one of the highest priorities for many organizations. Many efforts fail because leaders do not take into account the human factor in implementing change. Employees need help to master change and move from resistance to change by exploring the possibilities that change can bring for them. You can help employees cope with change by helping them develop a new vision for themselves, accept the losses, and explore the new possibilities that change can offer. The following tips can help you in coaching others to manage change:

- Acknowledge that resistance is often a process that people need to go through. Have employees list the sabotaging core beliefs or self-talk that may be operating.

- Help employees acknowledge the losses in change and look for the gains. For example, the next time they resist, have them spend time brainstorming both the losses and the gains brought by this change.

- Guide employees in determining what they have control over and what they do not.

- Help employees see that even though they can't change the situation, they can change their attitude about it.

Helping Employees Get in Charge of Their Self-Talk

A frequently quoted line from the movie *Field of Dreams*—"If you build it, they will come"—suggests the idea that people fulfill both their dreams and their nightmares. You can be a great role model and coach for employees, helping them become more optimistic, motivated, and resilient by helping them develop affirmative, realistic, and optimistic thoughts. You can also be a mirror for them when they magnify their faults and succumb to their fears.

You can help employees develop more positive self-talk by the doing the following:

- Being a good role model by demonstrating an attitude of curiosity and by receiving feedback from employees in a nondefensive manner.

- Expressing gratitude and appreciation for employees in a regular and continuous way and making sure you give as many kudos as criticisms.

- Challenging employees when they have distorted perceptions and helping them reframe their negative self-talk using the technique for refuting negative self-talk presented in Chapter 4.

Intercultural Literacy—Reading Others Accurately

Employees often find themselves derailed because they misunderstand or react negatively to the behavior of others. You can help them overcome this obstacle by showing them how to decode the meaning of others' behavior and deal with it less judgmentally.

Helping Employees Understand the Cultural Whys Behind Behaviors

When you see that an employee is confused or irritated by cultural differences, you can help by getting the individual to consider other possible meanings of the behavior. Ask the employee to list the specific behaviors, such as giving a soft handshake or not making eye contact, that are difficult to deal with. Ask what the behavior means to the employee. Then ask what it might mean to the person doing the behavior. At this point in the conversation you can add information that you have learned from your own experiences and from previous chapters in this book. In addition to providing information, you need to help the individual get to the heart of the frustration. The employee needs knowledge about differing cultural norms added to introspection about why these behaviors are irritating in order to increase understanding and improve interpersonal relationships.

Helping Employees See the Upsides and Downsides of All Cultural Norms

Coach the individual in moving beyond a narrow ethnocentric view by involving him in considering both the upsides and downsides of his own behavior and that of others. Ask the person to think of one of his important preferences or norms on the job, for example, being on time or staying until the work is done, and then suggest a couple of downsides for each. Follow that conversation with one about some norms or preferences that the person finds irritating, for example, using BlackBerrys at meetings or arriving late to appointments. Then ask the individual to list a couple of advantages of each of these behaviors. Then have a discussion about the learnings. The employee will gain a broader perspective from looking at the downsides of his own preferences and the upsides of the preferences of others. When you help the individual apply learnings to real work situations and see how he might change to deal with some irritations more effectively, growth will come.

Helping Employees Transcend Their Own Perspectives and Show Empathy

When an employee is having a difficult time with the behavior of a co-worker, boss, or teammate, use the following process to get her to walk in the other's shoes. Ask her to imagine the life of the other individual and become that person for a few minutes. Have her explain the behavior from the other person's perspective, telling why the person does it, how it makes sense, and why it seems like the best thing to do. You can help in this discussion by suggesting additional reasons and by helping to broaden the employee's perspective about the other person. You might consider using some of the following questions to help the individual walk in another's shoes:

- What might be the motivation for the other person's behavior?

- What aspects of the other person's cultural software might be playing a role in his or her reactions?

- What aspects of the employee's cultural software also influence his or her reaction?

- What will the employee lose if he or she accepts or understands the other person's perspective?

- What will the employee lose if he or she doesn't?

Social Architecting—
Enrolling and Engaging Others

Engagement, ownership, and commitment are important words that describe ideal work environments. Everyone is an architect of that environment, and the suggestions in this section will help you assist others in developing this capacity to build their desired work environment.

Helping Employees Serve as Cultural Interpreters

This is a coaching process that takes place in stages. Individuals aren't necessarily born with these skills, but everyone has the capacity to learn them. Begin by asking your employee to look for patterns in situations where she has confusion, frustration, and a lack of clarity about how to interact with a co-worker or customer. Have the employee share some of these situations with you. Perhaps a situation involves learning to deal with a new hire from New York who moves and talks too fast for the more relaxed culture of a southern town. Perhaps it involves helping union and management personnel understand one another better, or helping those in their twenties and those in their sixties give up the stereotypes that dismiss the other generation as inadequate for one reason or another. As a cultural interpreter and coach, you can start by having people check their assumptions and see how they might be able to help teammates understand one another better and get beyond the "good guys versus the bad guys."

Sometimes, the coaching work may involve dealing with ethnic norms, for example, those of a new community of Brazilians, Russians, or Vietnamese who moved into your neighborhood. In this case, cultural interpreters can help employees learn to avoid cultural faux pas and misunderstandings. Ideally, you will be able to provide concrete information about a culture. Being knowledgeable about certain norms and practices enables you to help someone learn the norms of another group so the person misinterprets less and responds appropriately more often.

But sometimes, you may need to do bridge building where the answers may not be clear. In that case your coaching is best accomplished by asking questions. For example, you might say to someone in his twenties who is impatient with an older worker, "What possible reasons might explain why Theresa is averse to learning this new technology?" Follow that question with a few others:

- What might make her less afraid?

- When were you ever afraid in your life? How did you get beyond it?

- What are the pluses Theresa brings to this work group? What would we miss if she were not here?

You want to give information about cultural norms where it is appropriate, but being a cultural interpreter is about more than knowledge. It is also about a kind, compassionate, and understanding heart. At the end of the conversation about Theresa, this person in his twenties might be able to help other people of the same generation see Theresa differently, more patiently and with more understanding and respect. Just as important, Theresa should also be coached about why and how to find value in the people in their twenties whom she works with. You could ask questions that take her back to that time in her life, that show how the world has changed, and that highlight the gifts of youth such as energy, curiosity, and vitality to help put a human face on that generation. Theresa can then help other people in their sixties be more patient with whatever bothers them about the younger generation, and both groups might see it as a rare and wonderful opportunity to expand their view and connect the two generations somewhere in the middle.

Helping Employees Communicate Effectively and Resolve Conflicts in Diverse Settings

First see how your employees describe their own communication style, giving them a chance to assess what works for them and what gets in the way. Your feedback will be a helpful addition to the learning process. Then create a plan for improvement that involves monthly check-ins. Suggest a log or journal that highlights interactions that went extremely well and those that were disappointing. In the check-ins, focus on the good news and bad, as well as new opportunities for growth. End each coaching session by having the individual identify an area of development for the month. For example, the individual might say, "I need to be more patient" or "I want to really listen better and not be distracted while someone is talking to me." As your coaching relationship grows, you and the employee can jointly agree after each conversation about where to put energy for improvement. Any unobtrusive observations you can make over the month may also help. If you see anything noteworthy, whether it is positive or negative, harvest those examples for the employee's learning. You may want to save this observation for the monthly session or discuss it in real time when you have the chance. In any case, paying attention and heightening the employee's awareness about being on your radar screen is not only an act of caring, it is an act of great coaching.

You can also coach the employee in using the four-step Heart-of-the-Matter Conversation process described in Chapter 6. Coach your employee on how to use it so it becomes second nature. The first time or two that the employee uses it, you can guide her with responses at each stage. By the third time you go through this process in the coaching role, you are merely an attentive listener who weighs in only when the person gets stuck. Your goal in all your coaching is autonomy.

Helping Employees Structure Synergistic and Compelling Environments

You coach most effectively when you function like a choir that sings the same refrain over and over. The refrain is this: "Our work group will only be as good as each one of us makes it. Every single person here has a responsibility to be kind, ethical, committed to our work and to each other, accountable, honest, and open to learning and growing."

Using the introspective process you learned in Chapter 3, you essentially hold up a mirror and ask each employee, one-on-one, what he or she is contributing to this group. Some sample questions to begin the conversation are

- How is this group or team different because you are a part of it?

- What environment do you want to create?

- How are your actions getting us closer to a stated goal?

- What must you bring to the environment to make it extraordinary, and what do you want from others to make this an ideal place to work?

- Everyone has unique gifts. What are yours? What are those of others?

- What do you need from others in order to be at your best?

Success in Coaching the Individual

Coaching is about dialogue and conversation so that each individual feels a commitment and responsibility to bring the best efforts to work every day. It is about conscious intervening in the life of the group to make it better, one person at a time. And, of course, the most important thing you do as a coach is model every single one of these synergistic behaviors you are seeking. People don't expect perfection, but they do want their leaders to be real. If you make mistakes, own them. Harvest the learning, share the psychic rewards as they are earned, and let people know how much they matter.

Time. Attention. Respect. Living and modeling the behaviors you are advocating will be your best coaching.

8

Coaching Teams for Emotional Intelligence in Your Diverse Workplace

Teams as well as individuals need to develop emotional intelligence skills that help enhance teamwork, improve group dynamics, and ultimately increase performance. You can stimulate this development by using the following activities with your team.

Affirmative Introspection — Taking a Look Inside

Team members can create synergy and nurture one another's creative spirit. Or they can maintain rigid, stereotypical perspectives about one another that prevent the team's overall effectiveness. Identifying team members' stereotypes and hot buttons will encourage growth and productive work relationships.

Helping the Team Know What Makes It Tick

Developing a team atmosphere where curiosity and nondefensive attitudes dominate is a desirable goal for most leaders. You can help the team establish norms that enable it to become more introspective and affirming by using the following techniques:

- Begin staff meetings by checking with each member to see how the person is doing and feeling at work. You can use quick warm-ups such as a word or phrase that expresses how each person feels about the week's accomplishments and that expresses where the person is at the moment. Or you might ask team members to share the best and worst thing that has happened to them during the past week.

▪ Have members share their work challenges in an introspective way. Using the introspective process from Chapter 3, ask team members to indicate why the challenge is important, what some impacts of the challenge are, how they feel about it, and what learnings they have gotten from dealing with it.

▪ Make time on a routine basis for the team to assess its own effectiveness, and be willing to comment on the team's dynamics or processes in a nonjudgmental way. For example, ask them to rate on a scale of 1 to 5 (with 1 low and 5 high) their satisfaction with their process in completing a recent project. Have team members share their ratings and discuss their perceptions. End by having each team member suggest one thing that could improve both product and process next time.

Helping the Team Be More Comfortable in Its Own Skin

Work teams become more synergistic and effective when trust among the members allows for risk taking and creativity. You can help the team develop comfort among themselves in the following ways:

▪ Establish ground rules that encourage safety and develop a common team vision.

▪ Develop a clear understanding of what constitutes a respectful environment. To do this, guide team members in using the pyramid technique explained in Chapter 6 to discuss and define their desired work environment.

▪ Use activities during some staff meetings in which the objective is to help members know one another better.

▪ Teach respectful ways to provide feedback and encourage openness by institutionalizing 360-degree feedback and using feedback sessions as a tool for development.

Helping the Team Be Aware of Its Own Biases and Hot Buttons

Diverse work teams can be synergistic and creative, but the more diverse the team, the more susceptible the members are to biases and hot buttons. In genuine relationships, conflict and annoying behavior are unavoidable. Effective teams have a commitment to talk openly about these issues and to resolve their conflicts in constructive ways. You can help your team be in tune with its own biases and hot buttons using the following techniques:

- Help team members be honest and open in identifying situations in which diverse conflicts and hot buttons are affecting them. You might have a regular "ouch time" at each meeting when members can bring up issues that could lead to conflict.

- Help team members identify their personality and work style preferences and explore areas of potential conflict with others. Using questionnaires that help team members understand one another's styles can be helpful.

- Help team members identify and share behaviors that might be the source of irritation for themselves and others.

Self-Governance—Getting a Handle on Your Feelings

These are times of great uncertainty, so it is little wonder that team members are unwilling to embrace change and at times sabotage new initiatives. Self-governance skills will help team members support one another as they experience emotions elicited by today's pluralistic, ever-changing society.

Helping the Team Make Ambiguity an Ally

One aspect of group dynamics is called "group think," which is the pressure that group members often feel to agree and achieve consensus. At times this pressure to come to a quick agreement comes with a high cost because it prevents the group from using the ambiguity of the situation to allow for synergistic, creative solutions. You can help your team be more effective if you coach team members to tolerate ambiguity using the following techniques:

- Help team members engage in a debate without coming to a final conclusion. Push them beyond either/or solutions and ask them to discuss multiple options.

- Teach the process of brainstorming ideas, in which team members generate as many ideas as possible without censorship and without judgment.

- Use the "Mental Board Members" technique described in Chapter 4 when the team is grappling with an ambiguous situation.

Helping the Team Become a Change Master

Leaders are often change agents and implementers of change. Therefore, you need to encourage the team to be open to the changes that leaders need to implement. You can help team members navigate through the process of change by using the following techniques:

- Help team members identify gains and losses as a group when they are facing difficult changes.

- Help team members identify a new vision for the group that the change will represent, focusing on how the team will function within the new reality.

- Involve team members in the planning and implementation of the change by getting their input and using their suggestions.

- Communicate clearly the reasons why the change is needed and desired.

- Help members navigate through the change process by identifying controllable aspects and specific actions they can take.

Helping the Team Get in Charge of Its Self-Talk

Like individuals, teams have collective inner narratives or self-talk stories. Stories such as "We are a resilient group," "We are the champions," or "Our diversity is our formula for success" could be productive. Other stories, such as "The good old days were the best," "People with diverse backgrounds don't belong here," or "The new reality is very depressing. We are doomed to fail" could be destructive. You can help your group develop more positive self-talk and challenge their pessimistic, unrealistic self-talk by using the following techniques:

- Guide them through the process of creating a vision and mission statement that is inclusive and empowering.

- Help them develop a group tagline that will foster optimism.

- Develop group norms by which members express their gratitude for one another. For example, end a meeting with a "symbolic toast" in which each team member toasts a colleague to the left or right (or both) for something that person has brought to the team or a way in which the individual has helped in the past month.

- Challenge the group's self-talk messages by reframing them in a positive way. Have the team identify the three most negative self-talk messages operating in the group and come up with more realistic and accurate messages to replace them.

Intercultural Literacy—Reading Others Accurately

Team members often find themselves locked into inaccurate and limiting assumptions about or judgmental reactions to the behavior of teammates and colleagues in other groups. You can help them overcome the misleading and hindering views by guiding them through activities that develop their intercultural literacy.

Helping the Team Understand the Cultural Whys Behind Behavior

Team members can work more effectively with one another and with those they serve if they correctly decode and do not misinterpret behaviors. You can help them in this process by asking them to share their favorite proverb. You can prime the pump by suggesting a few yourself, such as "The early bird gets the worm," Don't judge a book by its cover," "He who hesitates is lost," and "Fools rush in where angels fear to tread." Once they have their proverbs in mind, ask each person to share the proverb with the team along with the value that underlies it. Once all have shared, lead a group discussion about how those values play out on the team and affect interactions and performance. Then discuss how those values might influence behavior and communication in the group. For example, the value of caution may help the team be diligent in gathering all the facts before they proceed with a project; or the value of risk taking may make the group more tolerant of failures as long as they can learn from them. Also discuss how knowing what each team member values helps in positioning feedback they would give one another. Finally, have them write a proverb that is representative of some of the values of the team. For example, "The team is where the heart is," "A risk-free team is not worth being on," or "Healthy fruit comes from strong roots."

Helping the Team See the Upsides and Downsides of All Cultural Norms

Team performance is enhanced and relationships are strengthened when team members increase their sensitivity to the impact of their behavior on others in the group. Ask team members to make a list of three norms or preferences each brings. Then ask them to list the ways these benefit the team and the ways each norm can be overdone and hinder the group. For example, a preference for a strict adherence to schedules may help meet deadlines and not waste time, but it may also limit creativity in a rush for completion so that the team meets a deadline but misses the objective. Have team members share these preferences with the group and then discuss their learnings and how they can apply these to the team's processes.

Helping the Team Transcend Its Own Perspective and Show Empathy

Teams are hindered when they take a judgmental and adversarial stance in dealing with other work groups. When one team is experiencing difficulty with another team or department, try the following.

Divide the team into two groups and have half take the part of their own team and the other half take the part of the "difficult" team or department. Give each group time to discuss how they see the situation and why they act and react the way they do. Then have each group explain the situation from its perspective. Once the groups have heard each other, ask each to take five minutes to discuss in their small group what they heard and then tell the other group what they heard. Then lead a total group discussion about their learnings and insights into ways to resolve the problem.

Social Architecting — Enrolling and Engaging Others

Social Architecting fosters joy, human connection, and a sense of belonging in the workplace. The skills used here increase understanding between team members and are the ticket to high spirits and mutual support.

Helping the Team Serve as a Cultural Interpreter

Interpersonal understanding is essential on a team. It engenders commitment, support, and loyalty. This understanding may not happen by itself but requires building bridges with others. The suggestions presented here will help you develop this ability on your team.

In a large group, have people brainstorm some of the behaviors they identify as resulting in miscommunication and lack of connection between members of the team. Maybe the behavior is people always coming late to meetings; maybe it is people not speaking English even though they know how to do so and making others feel left out. Those who make suggestions and observations in the brainstorming are not necessarily talking about their own realities or observations, and not everyone has to agree with each perception. You want people's realities to be on that flip chart, but everyone's view counts, and there does not need to be consensus on perceptions.

Then in groups of not more than four people, have each individual within the small group select one of the situations that is both relevant and difficult to deal with. The goal is to be able to reinterpret or reframe that difficult or problematic situation. The group essentially serves as the cultural interpreter to the person with the difficulty and helps him or her expand the viewpoint and feel the points of connection. One at a time, in round-robin fashion, each person gets help with realizing that a cultural dilemma can be viewed differently.

It always depends on the person's vantage point. The end result is a kinder, gentler interpretation of one's own issue, based in part on new understanding and information. The best part of the round robin is that it leaves team members with the skill and ability of giving information and perspective to others so that team members really do learn how to function as interpreters for one another.

Helping the Team Communicate Effectively and Resolve Conflicts in Diverse Settings

A primary criterion for an effective team is how it deals with the inevitable conflicts that arise. To help the team deal with conflict, try the following.

In a group setting or meeting, use subgroups to have team members identify the areas of conflict that are most destructive to the cohesion and productivity of the group. As a manager, you will be the facilitator of this process. In small groups you are providing a degree of anonymity for people who, because of individual style or ethnic cultural influences, do not feel comfortable calling out the particular areas of conflict.

Using small groups to talk about what members observe is an easier way for people to bring up a problem. Once the small group data from every group is listed on a flip chart, you can ask for volunteers to use the Heart of the Matter Conversation from Chapter 6 in front of the whole group. Using anonymous conflicts, no one feels the need for protection. You are providing safety, group learning, collaboration, and a chance for individual and collective skill building. By demonstrating two rounds publicly, employees will get the knack of how to do it. Then have people divide into pairs and identify and use a situation that is real for them. Encourage them to use the most urgent, real situation they are facing.

To increase trust and openness on the team, you can suggest that members give and get feedback, taking the necessary time. Both options are available to you and you may choose one at any given time. At a team meeting have them give feedback to one another using the following statements:

1. A clear strength of ours as a team in communicating is . . .

2. My dominant mode or style of communicating is . . .

3. I intend this style to be helpful to the team in the following ways . . .

4. We can strengthen our effectiveness if we learn to style shift by doing more of . . . and doing less of . . .

Have a whole-group discussion of what team members learned and how they will apply this knowledge to how the team operates.

Helping the Team Structure Synergistic and Compelling Environments

Begin by having your work group construct its ideal environment, and by the time it finishes, they will have created the desired norms for the team. Have team members focus on two aspects: the task, or how they actually get the work done, and the relationship, the soft side, or the power of emotion and its connection to commitment, follow-through, and emotional support. In short, the soft side is the part that looks at how team members treat one another.

The questions you want to explore with the team are the following:

1. What do you want to see on this team in both the task and relationship arenas?

2. What do you as a team member need from others? What are you willing to give?

3. What single behavior, if accomplished in the task arena, would propel the group to greater heights?

4. What relationship behavior, if missing, would cause employees to want to leave the unit?

Engaging the team in this conversation, and others like it, will not be a quick process. Have team members write the answers to these questions for themselves first, and let them know ahead of time that there will be a respectful, important conversation in the whole group dealing with the answers to the four questions.

Success in Coaching the Team

In these processes you are a manager functioning as a facilitator. You are the catalyst that leads the team into this discussion, and you or a team member record everyone's responses on flip charts. Once the responses are public, you can lead the discussion about what to make of the information and how to use it. To create sustainability in this environment, the group needs to articulate its norms. Help the group develop an appropriate list of team ground rules from this discussion.

The process requires that you and everyone else present be open to taking the data where it goes. You will not be effective if your expectations are preset and you are trying to lead people to say what you want. As surprising as that statement may be, it is needed because we have seen the process violated many times and team members inadvertently set up to give particular answers. This process should give you and the team conversation that is both real and substantive. It should also plant the realization in team members that soft skills have hard consequences. A set of norms that you all agree to, which encompasses ways to hold one another accountable and create ownership, is worth gold. Is this team and this organization theirs? Is it going to flourish? If it does, they will make it so.

The writer Terry McMillan has said, "Can't nothin' make your life work if you ain't the architect." For teams, we would adapt her quote to say, "Can't nothin' make our unit work if we ain't the architects."

Afterword

The importance of dealing effectively with feelings about differences has never been more urgent than it is at this time in human history. We know from personal experience, our own and our clients', that framing your world through the Emotional Intelligence and Diversity Model, and using the skills you learned in this book, can be transformational and life changing. We have shared our approach with you in the context of mirrors and maps. We hope that through the explanations, concepts, examples, and action-steps, you continue to use the mirrors to understand yourself better and follow the maps to greater effectiveness, satisfaction, and peace in your professional life.

Notes

Chapter 1

1. Tony Simons, "The High Cost of Lost Trust," *Harvard Business Review,* September 2002.
2. R. E. Boyatzis, Presentation, Linkage Conference on Emotional Intelligence, Chicago, September 27, 1999.
3. L. M. Spencer Jr. and S. Spencer, *Competency at Work: Models for Superior Performance* (New York: John Wiley and Sons, 1993); and L. M. Spencer, D. C. McClelland, and S. M. Spencer, *Competency Assessment Methods: History and State of the Art* (Boston: Hay/McBer, 1997).
4. A. Pesuric and W. Bigham, "The New Look in Behavior Modeling," *Training and Development,* July 1996, 25–33.

Chapter 3

1. Daniel Goleman, *Emotional Intelligence: Why It Can Matter More than IQ* (New York: Bantam, 1997), 10–14; and Joseph Le Doux, "What Is Emotional Intelligence?" found at www.brainconnection.com/topics/?main=fa/emotionalintelligence2 (accessed May 1, 2008).

Chapter 4

1. Abraham H. Maslow, *Motivation and Personality* (New York: Harper, 1954).
2. M. M. Lombardo and C. D. McCauley, *The Dynamics of Management Derailment,* Technical report no. 34 (Greensborough, NC: Center for Creative Leadership, 1988).
3. Martin Seligman, *Authentic Happiness: Using the New Positive Psychology to Realize Your Potential for Lasting Fulfillment* (New York: Free Press, 2002), 120.

Chapter 5

1. Geert Hofstede, "National Cultures and Corporate Cultures," in *Communication Between Cultures,* edited by L. A. Samovar and R. E. Porter (Belmont, CA: Wadsworth, 1984).

Index